MW01491130

Write a review to receive any *free* eBook from our Catalog - $99 Value!

If you recently bought this book we would love to hear from you! Benefit from receiving a free eBook from our catalog at http://www.emereo.org/ if you write a review on Amazon (or the online store where you purchased this book) about your last purchase!

How does it work?

To post a review on Amazon, just log in to your account and click on the Create your own review button (under Customer Reviews) of the relevant product page. You can find examples of product reviews in Amazon. If you purchased from another online store, simply follow their procedures.

What happens when I submit my review?

Once you have submitted your review, send us an email at review@emereo.org with the link to your review, and the eBook you would like as our thank you from http://www.emereo.org/. Pick any book you like from the catalog, up to $99 RRP. You will receive an email with your eBook as download link. It is that simple!

Table of Contents

1 Problem Management

Goals and Objectives

Problem Management is responsible for managing lifecycle of all problems. The primary objectives of Problem Management are:

- To prevent problems and resulting incidents from happening
- To eliminate recurring incidents
- To minimize the impact of incidents that cannot be prevented.

Scope

Clear distinction should be made between the purpose, scope and activities of Problem Management and those of Incident Management. In many cases staff may not clearly understand the distinction, and as a result not utilize their efforts in the most effective and efficient manner.

What is the difference between Incident Management and Problem Management?

Analogy: *If our gardens and lawns were affected by weeds, how would we address the situation?*

Incident Management: Use techniques that address the symptoms but still allow the weeds to grow back: (e.g. Pull them out, mow over them, use a hedge-trimmer, and buy a goat).

Problem Management: Use techniques that address the root-cause of the symptoms, so that weeds will no longer grow. (E.g. Use poison, dig roots out, re-lawn, concrete over etc.)

This is a simple explanation showing the difference between Incident Management and Problem Management. Incident Management is not concerned with the root cause, and only addresses the symptoms as quickly as possible. Problem Management however takes a long-term focus and approach in order to prevent the symptoms (weeds) from occurring again.

For most implementations of Problem Management the scope includes:

- The activities required to diagnose the root cause of incidents and to determine the resolution to those problems
- Activities that ensure that the resolution is implemented through the appropriate control procedures, usually through interfaces with Change Management and Release & Deployment Management
- Proactive activities that eliminate errors in the infrastructure before they result in incidents and impact on the business and end users.

Benefits

Problem Management should be used in coordination with Incident and Change Management processes to ensure service availability and quality are improved. When incidents are resolved, information about the resolution is recorded. Over time this organizational learning is used to speed up the resolution time and identify permanent solutions.

Other benefits of Problem Management include:

- Higher availability of IT services
- Higher productivity of business and IT staff
- Reduced expenditure on workarounds or fixes that do not work
- Reduction in duplicated costs and effort in fire-fighting or resolving repeat incidents.

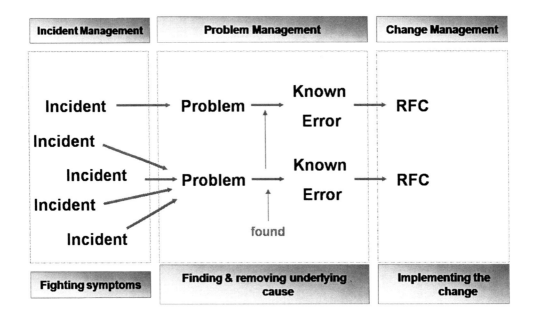

The basic concepts of Problem Management

Problem Management Activities

The activities of Problem Management are divided into two major sub-processes:

- Reactive Problem Management: typically driven by the identification of repeat or major incidents, and executed within the role of Service Operation
- Proactive Problem Management: which is initiated in Service Operation, but generally managed and driven by Continual Service Improvement.

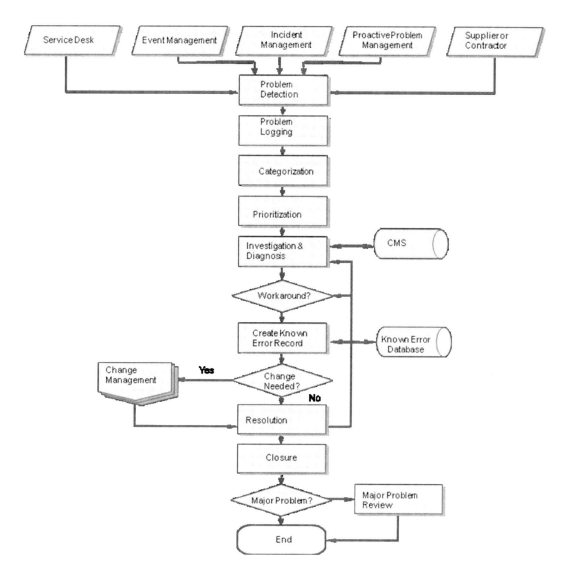

Typical activities of Problem Management

© Crown Copyright 2007 Reproduced under license from OGC

Overview of Reactive Problem Management activities:

1. Problem detection
2. Problem logging
3. Problem categorization
4. Problem investigation and diagnosis
5. Workarounds
6. Raising a Known Error record
7. Problem resolution
8. Problem closure
9. Major Problem reviews.

1. Problem detection

The detection of problems can occur in multiple ways, so planning for the implementation of Problem Management should consider what interfaces need to be developed to cater for these various sources. Typically these include:

- Problems detected as a result of multiple incidents that have been raised by automated means (under the control of Event Management)
- Problems detected at the Service Desk based on a large volume of like high impact incidents, requiring a problem to be logged straight away
- Problems detected by the Service Desk or other technical support groups based on incident investigation
- Problems detected as a result of external suppliers notifying of errors in the infrastructure/applications under their control

- Trend analysis of incidents, found as part of the execution of Proactive Problem Management.

2. Problem logging

Like incidents, all detected problems (regardless of source) must be recorded with a unique reference number and be date/time stamped to enable full historical tracking, control and escalation. Where possible, the same service management tools should be used to record incident and problem records, so that any relevant details can be copied/referenced from incidents to associated problems.

Normally this will include such details as:
- User details
- Service details
- Equipment details
- Date/time of recording
- Categorization and priority details
- Incident descriptions/symptoms
- Details of actions taken.

3. Problem categorization

To ensure consistency and allow for effective matching, detection and reporting, both incidents and problems should be categorized in the same away. Multi-level categorization is typically used, where the service management tool is populated with up to three of four levels of category details.

.Copyright The Art of Service | Brisbane, Australia | Email:service@theartofservice.com
Web: http://theartofservice.com | eLearning: http://theartofservice.org | Phone: +61 (0)7 3252 2055

Over time, continual improvement should seek for ways in which to improve the categorization techniques used.

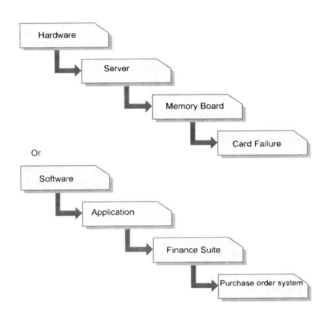

Multi-level problem categorization

© Crown Copyright 2007 Reproduced under license from OGC

4. Problem prioritization

While incidents and problems will have similar elements to their priority coding systems, problem prioritization will also take into account the frequency and impact of the related incidents. This is important in order to give involved staff some understanding of the relative severity of problems, and what level of response and investigation is required.

Due to the long term focus of Problem Management, prioritization will also consider the severity of the problem from an infrastructure perspective, including:

- Can the system be recovered, or does it need to be replaced?
- How much will it cost?
- How many people, with what skills, will be needed to fix the problem?
- How long will it take to fix the problem?
- How extensive is the problem (e.g. how many CIs are affected)?

Depending on the nature and severity of the problem, it may require a single person, small group or dedicated problem investigation team, so priority needs to be assigned correctly to initiate the appropriate response.

5. Problem investigation and diagnosis

Problem Management should coordinate an investigation to try to diagnose the root cause of the problem. The speed and nature of this investigation will vary depending upon the impact, severity and urgency of the problem. Like Incident Management, the Configuration Management System should be used to help assess the level of impact and to assist in diagnosing the exact point of failure.

Where necessary, recreating the failure in a test environment can assist in determining reason(s) for disruption and then to try various solutions to the problem in a safe and control manner.

To do this effectively without causing further disruption to the users, a test environment that mirrors the production environment is required.

Brainstorming is often an activity that occurs at this stage, involving all appropriate IT staff, customers and suppliers to collectively gain intelligence and ideas. Many research studies have been performed into other effective techniques that assist in the analysis, diagnosis and resolution of problems. Some of the most widely used techniques include:

Kepner and Tregoe

Charles Kepner and Benjamin Tregoe developed a method for analyzing problems. Their theory states that Problem analysis should be a systematic process of Problem solving and should take maximum advantage of knowledge and experience. They distinguish the following five phases for Problem analysis:

1. Defining the Problem
2. Describing the Problem with regard to identity, location, time and size
3. Establishing possible causes
4. Testing the most probable cause
5. Verifying the true cause.

Depending on time and available information, these phases can be applied with various levels of effort and resources.

Pareto Analysis

Pareto analysis is a very simple technique that helps you to choose the most effective changes to make. It uses the Pareto principle – the idea that by doing 20% of work you can generate 80% of the advantage of doing the entire job. Pareto analysis is a formal technique for finding the changes that will give the biggest benefits. It is useful where many possible courses of action are competing for your attention, in this case where multiple solutions exist for an identified problem, or when choosing which problem to address first.

To use the Pareto analysis technique:

1. List the problems you face, or the options you have available
2. Group options where they are facets of the same larger problem
3. Apply an appropriate score to each group
4. Work on the group with the highest score

Ishikawa Diagrams

Ishikawa diagrams were proposed by Kaoru Ishikawa in the 1960s, initially used to improve quality management processes in the Kawasaki shipyards, and in the process became one of the founding fathers of modern management. It is known as a fishbone diagram because of its shape, similar to the side view of a fish skeleton.

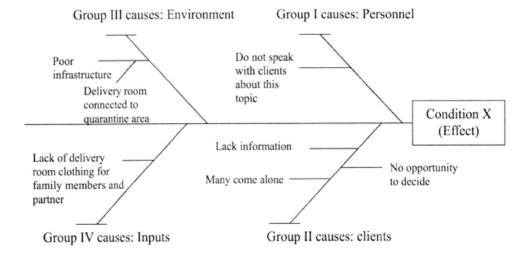

Group III causes: Environment — Group I causes: Personnel

Poor infrastructure

Delivery room connected to quarantine area

Do not speak with clients about this topic

Condition X (Effect)

Lack of delivery room clothing for family members and partner

Lack information

Many come alone

No opportunity to decide

Group IV causes: Inputs — Group II causes: clients

Example of an Ishikawa diagram used for Problem Management

An Ishikawa diagram is typically the result of a brainstorming session in which members of a group offer ideas on how to improve a product, process or service. The main goal is represented by the trunk of the diagram, and primary factors are represented as branches. Secondary factors are then added as stems, and so on. Creating the diagram stimulates discussion and often leads to increased understanding of a complex Problem.

Pain Value Analysis

This technique adopts a broader view of the impact caused by an incident/problem, where a more in-depth analysis determines exactly what level of pain has been caused to the organization/business involved.

The development of a formula that can calculate this pain level is required, which often includes such factors as:

- The number of people affected
- The duration of the downtime caused
- The cost to the business (if this can be effectively modeled).

Chronological Analysis

This technique analyses all of the events and actions that have occurred in order to see the relationship between them, or to discount any which should not be associated in the series. This requires consistent recording and documentation so that an accurate timeline of events can be understood.

5. Workarounds

While investigation into the root cause of problems and the development of appropriate solutions is still being undertaken, effort should be made as to how workarounds might be used to reduce the user/business impact until the permanent resolution is available. Workarounds are best defined as a set of predefined steps to take as a means of reducing or eliminating the impact of an Incident or a Problem (e.g. restarting a failed Configuration Item). Workarounds for Problems are documented with the Known Error records in the Known Error Database (KEDB).

Although workarounds can be developed by any involved party (Service Desk analysts, technical specialists or external suppliers), they should be analyzed by Problem Management before being formally recorded in the

KEDB. Where workarounds do provide temporary relief from the associated symptoms and impact, it is important to continue to track any related incidents so that future effort and resources in developing a permanent solution can be justified.

6. Raising a Known Error record

So that effective matching can occur, a Known Error record should be created within the KEDB as soon as the diagnosis is complete (and/or a valid workaround has been identified). This improves the visibility of the information required to match associated incidents and to find appropriate workarounds as a temporary means to overcoming disruption.

Where there is some benefit to creating a Known Error record earlier in the Problem Management process (i.e. before diagnosis is complete), it can be created as soon as it becomes useful to do so. In these cases, any further actions performed during its investigation and diagnosis would subsequently be captured.

7. Problem resolution

When a successful resolution has been identified and tested, approval should be sought for its implementation to the production (live) environment. Depending on the nature and scope of service management already in place and resolution to be implemented, this typically involves raising a Request for Change (RFC) for approval, either by a Change Advisory Board (CAB), or Emergency CAB for serious and urgent issues. Once the appropriate Change evaluation and authorization has occurred, the change should be scheduled according to normal Change and Release policy requirements. There may be some problems for which a Business Case for resolution cannot be justified (e.g. where the impact is limited but the cost of resolution would be extremely high). In such cases, a decision may be taken to leave the Problem Record open but to use a workaround description in the Known Error Record to detect and resolve any recurrences quickly.

8. Problem closure

When any changes and post implementation reviews have been successfully completed, and the resolution has proved to be effective, the problem record should be formally closed, with an update made to any associated incident records that are still open. This closure activity should also check that all required fields and documentation items are complete, and that the status has been updated to reflect the successful resolution of the error.

9. Major Problem reviews

The priority coding system used for Problem Management should provide special distinction for Major Problems. Like Major Incidents, these are problems with the highest level of impact (see Problem prioritization) that result in major business/organizational disruption. After successfully implementing solutions to a Major Problem, a review should be conducted in order to assess:

- What was done correctly?
- What was done wrong?
- What could be done better in the future?
- Could this problem/error be replicated in any other portion of the infrastructure?
- Was there any third-party responsibility?
- Are there any follow-up actions needed?

Such reviews are an important pass of continual improvement, with any lessons learned being documented in appropriate procedures, work instructions, diagnostic scripts or Known Error Records. The Problem Manager facilitates the session and documents any agreed actions.

The knowledge learned from the review should be incorporated into a service review meeting with the business customer to ensure the customer is aware of the actions taken and the plans to prevent future major incidents from occurring. This helps to improve customer satisfaction and assure the business that Service Operations is handling major incidents responsibly and actively working to prevent their future recurrence.

Proactive Problem Management

The three main activities that normally make up the sub-process of Proactive Problem Management are:

1. Major Problem Reviews *(see Major Problem reviews)*

2. Trend Analysis
- Review reports from other processes (e.g. trends in incidents, availability levels, relationships with changes and releases)
- Identify recurring Problems or training opportunities for IT staff, customers and end users.

3. Targeting Preventative Action
- Perform a cost-benefit analysis of all costs associated with prevention
- Target specific areas taking up the most support attention
- Coordinate preventative action with Availability and Capacity Management, focusing on vulnerable areas of the infrastructure (e.g. single points of failure, components reaching full capacity/utilization).

Managing Known Errors from the Service Transition Phase

It is likely that during the testing of new applications, systems or releases a prioritization system will be used to eradicate the more serious faults. However, it is possible that minor faults are not rectified – often because of the balance that has to be made between delivering new functionality to the business as quickly as possible and ensuring totally fault-free code or components.

Where a decision is made to release something into the production environment that includes known deficiencies, these should be logged as Known Errors in the KEDB, together with details of workarounds or resolution activities. There should be a formal step in the testing sign-off that ensures that this handover always takes place.

History indicates that if this does not happen, it will lead to far higher support costs when the users start to experience the faults and raise incidents that have to be re-diagnosed and resolved from the beginning again.

Triggers and Interfaces

When viewed in the context of Service Operations, the majority of problem records will be raised as a result of one or more incidents identified to be of a single root cause. This identification can occur in many ways, through formal and informal, manual and automated measures. Throughout the lifecycle of these problem records, information will be passed to and from Problem Management to assist in the effective and timely investigation, diagnosis and resolution of errors. In this context, the primary interfaces with Incident Management have already been discussed within chapters 6.2 & 6.3.

Other key interfaces that exist include:

- **Service Strategy**
  - *Financial Management* – for providing modeling of the business impact and financial cost of identified problems, including the development of a business case for their resolution.

- **Service Design**
  - *IT Service Continuity Management* – for providing guidance and measures as to the possible invocation of recovery mechanisms
  - *Service Level Management* – for providing feedback as to the customer impact of problems/Known Errors, and their general satisfaction with Problem Management
  - *Capacity Management* – for assisting with investigations into capacity and performance related problems
  - *Availability Management* – determining strategies for ways in which to improve availability and reduce downtime. Proactive Problem Management is a typical supported role, analyzing vulnerable areas of the infrastructure (e.g. single points of failure) to prevent future problems.

- **Service Transition**
  - *Change Management* – RFCs should be raised when requiring a change to controlled CIs in order to implement a permanent solution. Change Management should also review whether the change has delivered a successful solution to the problem/Known Error
  - *Release & Deployment* – Any Known Errors detected during the development and testing of new and modified services, systems and applications should be documented and communicated to Problem Management.

- o *Configuration Management* – The Configuration Management System (CMS) should be used to assist in the evaluation of impact for problems/Known Errors, and to provide historical tracking for the relationships between CIs, incidents, problems and Known Errors.

- **Continual Service Improvement**
  - o *CSI (7 Step) Improvement* Process – used to identify, coordinate and drive improvements, which may involve the documentation and resolution of problems/Known Errors.

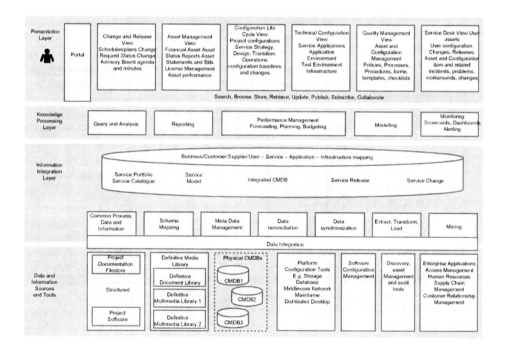

The Service Knowledge Management System

© Crown Copyright 2007 Reproduced under license from OGC

The Known Error Database (KEDB) should be interfaced with various elements of an organization's Service Knowledge Management System (SKMS) so that relationships can be created and understood between incidents, problems, known errors, CIs, changes and releases.

Key Performance Indicators (KPIs) for Problem Management

Measures that can be used to demonstrate the effectiveness and efficiency of the Problem Management process include:

- The number of problems grouped by status (open, closed, known errors etc)
- The number of RFCs created by Problem Management
- The number of workarounds developed for Known Errors and incidents
- The percentage of incidents resolved at first contact (should be increasing)
- The average time to resolve incidents (should be decreasing)
- The average time to close problems
- Customer satisfaction levels
- Average costs for solving problems
- Number and percentage of problems that were resolved within SLA limits
- Percentage of incidents not linked to problems and known errors
- The number of major problem reviews conducted.

2 Problem Management Roles

Problem Manager

There should be a designated person (or, in larger organizations, a team) responsible for Problem Management. Smaller organizations may not be able to justify a full-time resource for this role, and it can be combined with other roles in such cases, but it is essential that it not just be left to technical resources to perform. There needs to be a single point of coordination and an owner of the Problem Management process. This role will coordinate all Problem Management activities and will have specific responsibility for:

- Liaison with all problem resolution groups to ensure swift resolution of problems within SLA targets
- Ownership and protection of the KEDB
- Gatekeeper for the inclusion of all Known Errors and management or search algorithms
- Formal closure of all Problem Records
- Liaison with suppliers, contractors, etc. to ensure that third parties fulfill their contractual obligations, especially with regard to resolving problems and providing problem-related information and data
- Arranging, running, documenting and all follow-up activities relating to Major Problem Reviews.

Problem-Solving Groups

The actual solving of problems is likely to be undertaken by one or more technical support groups and/or suppliers or support contractors – under the coordination of the Problem Manager.

Where an individual problem is serious enough to warrant it, a dedicated problem management team should be formulated to work together in overcoming that particular problem. The Problem Manager has a role to play in making sure that the correct number and level of resources is available in the team and for escalation and communication up the management chain of all organizations concerned.

3 Implementing the Problem Management process

Typically the implementation of the Problem Management process comes from the identified need for formalized practices for delivering and supporting services in a controlled and efficient manner. There can be many types of approaches used for implementing this process, including those using project management methodologies, or those described in the lifecycle phase Continual Service Improvement. Even the practices from the Service Transition lifecycle phase themselves are useful guidance to consider when implementing these processes in an effective way.

3.1 The Continual Service Improvement Model

The CSI Model provides the basis by which improvements to Service Operation can be made. They are questions asked in order to ensure all the required elements are identified to achieve the improvements desired.

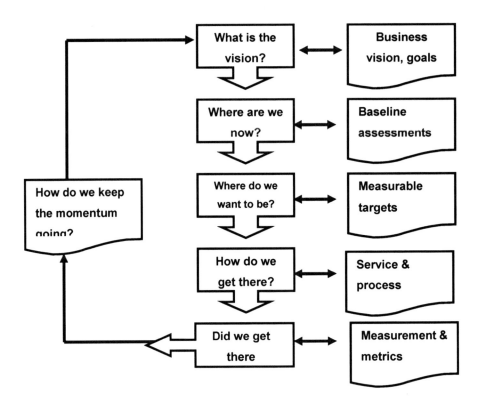

Continual Service Improvement Model

© Crown Copyright 2007 Reproduced under license from OGC

.Copyright The Art of Service │ Brisbane, Australia │ Email:service@theartofservice.com
Web: http://theartofservice.com │ eLearning: http://theartofservice.org │ Phone: +61 (0)7 3252 2055

The Continual Service Improvement Model summarizes the constant cycle for improvement. While there may be a focus on Service Operation, the questions require close interactions with all the other ITIL® processes in order to achieve Continual Service Improvement.

Steps taken to improve Service Operation

- **What is the Vision?** Defining what wants to be achieved by improving Service Operation. Is the focus on Service Quality, compliance, security, costs or customer satisfaction? What is the broad approach that we should take?

- **Where are we now?** Baselines taken by performing maturity assessments and by identifying what practices are currently being used (including informal and ad-hoc processes) What information can be provided by the Service Portfolio regarding strengths, weaknesses, risks and priorities of the Service Provider.

- **Where do we want to be?** Defining key goals and objectives that wish to be achieved by the formalization of Service Operation processes, including both short term and long term targets.

- **How do we get there?** Perform a gap analysis between the current practices and defined targets to begin developing plans to overcome these gaps. Typically the process owners and Service Operation manager will oversee the design/improvement of the processes, making sure they are fit for purpose and interface as needed with other Service Management processes.

- **Did we get there?** At agreed time schedules, checks should be made as to how the improvement initiatives have progressed. Which objectives have been achieved? Which haven't? What went well and what went wrong?

- **How do we keep the momentum going?** Now that the targets and objectives have been met, what is the next course of improvements that can be made? This should feed back into re-examining the vision and following the CSI model steps again.

4 Managing Cultural Change

Formalizing processes and procedures will require the delivery and management of cultural changes. History has shown that initiatives surrounding Service Operation, especially Incident and Problem Management, tend to create some resistance in the IT staff, customers and end users involved or affected. This is largely due to the perception of bottlenecks and bureaucracy being created, or the taking away of power and authority that the staff members may previously have had.

Those responsible or accountable for implementing Service Operation should consider the various stakeholders that will be involved or affected, and how best their support can be gained. This typically will involve holding awareness sessions, team meetings and face to face discussions, so that all those involved understand the reasons for the changes, the benefits that are being created and how their role contributes or has changed as a result.

5 Checklist for Problem Management practices

The following section provides common items that should be satisfied as when implementing the practices involved for Operational Support & Analysis.

Problem Management

- We have defined Problem Management's Purpose, Goal and Objective
- We have defined Problem Management's Scope
- We have defined Problem Management's Value to the business
- We have defined Problem Management's Policies, Principles and basic concepts
- The "Problem Detection" process activity is specified
- The "Problem Logging" process activity is specified
- The "Problem Categorization" process activity is specified
- The "Problem Prioritization" process activity is specified
- The "Problem Investigation and Diagnosis" process activity is specified
- The "Workarounds" process activity is specified
- The "Raising a known error record" process activity is specified
- The "Problem Resolution" process activity is specified
- The "Problem Closure" process activity is specified
- The "Major Problem Review" process activity is specified
- The "Errors detected in the development environment" process activity is specified

- We have defined Problem Management's Triggers, Inputs, Outputs and interfaces
- The CMS acts as a valuable source for Problem Management
- We have a Known Error Database to allow quicker diagnosis and resolution
- We have defined Problem Management's KPIs and metrics
- We have defined Problem Management's Information Management reporting
- We have defined Problem Management's Challenges, Critical Success Factors and Risks.

6 Supporting documents

Through the documents, look for text surrounded by << and >> these are indicators for you to create some specific text.

6.1 Business Justification Template

IT Services

Business Justification

Process: Problem Management

Status:	In draft	
	Under Review	
	Sent for Approval	
	Approved	
	Rejected	
Version:	<<your version>>	
Release Date:		

Business Justification Document for Problem Management

The document is not to be considered an extensive statement as its topics have to be generic enough to suit any reader for any organization. However, the reader will certainly be reminded of the key topics that have to be considered.

This document serves as a reference for HOW TO APPROACH THE TASK OF SEEKING FUNDS for the implementation of the Problem Management process.
This document provides a basis for completion within your own organization.

This document was;   Prepared by: _____   On: <<date>>   And accepted by: _____   On: <<date>>

Problem Management Business Justification

A strong enough business case will ensure progress and funds are made available for any IT initiative.

This may sound like a bold statement but it is true. As IT professionals we have (for too long) assumed that we miss out on funds while other functional areas (e.g. Human resources and other shared services) seem to get all that they want.

However, the problem is not with them, it's with US. We are typically poor salespeople when it comes to putting our case forward.

We try to impress with technical descriptions, rather than talking in a language that a business person understands.

For example:

We say	We should say
We have to increase IT security controls, with the implementation of a new firewall.	Two weeks ago our biggest competitor lost information that is now rumored to be available on the internet.
The network bandwidth is our biggest bottleneck and we have to go to a switched local environment.	The e-mail you send to the other national managers will take 4 to 6 hours to be delivered. It used to be 2 to 3 minutes, but we are now using our computers for many more tasks.

Changes to the environment are scheduled for a period of time when we expect there to be minimal business impact.	We are making the changes on Sunday afternoon. There will be less people working then.

Doesn't that sound familiar?

To help reinforce this point even further, consider the situation of buying a new fridge. What if the technically savvy sales person wants to explain "the intricacies of the tubing structure used to super cool the high pressure gases, which flow in an anti-clockwise direction in the Southern hemisphere".

Wouldn't you say "too much information, who cares – does it make things cold?"

Well IT managers need to stop trying to tell business managers about the tubing structure and just tell them what they are interested in.

So let's know look at some benefits of Problem Management. Remember that the comments here are generic, as they have to apply to any organization. If you need assistance in writing business benefits for your organization please e-mail service@theartofservice.com for a quotation.

Benefits	Notes/Comments/Relevance
Through a properly controlled and structured Problem Management process we will be able to more effectively align the delivery of IT service to the business requirements. This is achieved through the nature of the process by removing the underlying issues that the business people will have with incidents. There are clear links between this process and all others. A well run Problem Management process will ensure that the best returns on the investment made in implementation of structured processes is achieved.	
A heightened visibility and increased communication related to known error and problems to both business and IT support staff. The reader should be able to draw upon experience regarding the overall negative impact that an unpublicised problem or known error has. Also the negative moral impact on staff that have to deal with fallout from problems and known errors that they were not even aware of.	

Organizations and therefore IT environments are becoming increasingly complex and continually facing new challenges.

The ability to meet these challenges is dependant on the speed and flexibility of the organization. The ability to cope with more changes at the business level will be directly impacted by how well IT Departments can remove known errors so as to prevent repetitive loss of service due to recurring incidents.

(Reader, here you can describe a missed opportunity, due to slow Problem Management or a process dragged down by bureaucracy)

Noticeable increases in the **potential** productivity of end users and key personnel through less interruption, higher quality services and less diversion from planned tasks due to problems and known errors not being dealt with correctly.

The goal statement of Problem Management is to reduce the negative impact of Incidents, Problems and Errors. By the very nature of this statement we can expect less user interruptions. Whether end users and staff take advantage of this reduced down-time is not an issue for IT professionals to monitor. Knowing that we have made more working time available is what we need to publish – NOT productivity rates.

An ITIL Problem Management process will guide you towards understanding the financial implications of known errors.

This has real benefits as it may prevent an organization from starting a change then losing money later as they realize the funds are simply not available for completion or there was no reason to remove the known error in the first place.

Aides in improving the security aspects of the organization with respect to IT. This is because a security manager or security responsible person should be on the problem team, especially for major, high potential impact problems and known errors.	
The Problem Manager will ensure that the risks of the change to remove a known error have been fully assessed prior to starting the change. Risk assessment methodologies form part of other ITIL processes, but the Problem Manager has a responsibility of making sure that all potential impact areas have been addressed.	
With a sound Problem Management process we can expect an overall declining rate of incidents as more and more problems and known errors are being identified and removed.	
Any ITIL process has the potential to increase the credibility of the IT group, as they offer a higher quality of service, combined with an overall professionalism that can be lacking in ad-hoc activities.	

6.2 Objectives and Goals

IT Services

Detailed Objectives/Goals

Process: Problem Management

Status:	In draft Under Review Sent for Approval Approved Rejected	
Version:	<<your version>>	
Release Date:		

Detailed Objectives/Goals for Problem Management

The document is not to be considered an extensive statement as its topics have to be generic enough to suit any reader for any organization. However, the reader will certainly be reminded of the key topics that have to be considered.

The detailed objectives for Problem Management should include the following salient points:

Objective	Notes
To remove reoccurring Incidents from the IT Infrastructure. Reoccurring Incidents in the IT Infrastructure is a sure sign of the organisation being reactive and not having proactive processes in place.	Met/Exceeded/Shortfall ☺ ☺ ☹ Dates/names/role titles
Minimise the adverse affects of Incidents, Problems and Known Errors on the IT Infrastructure and the Business. Once developed a Problem Management process can be used to supply workarounds and solutions for Incidents, Problems, and Known Errors.	

To establish efficient assessment guidelines that cover the business, technical and financial aspects of removing Problems and Known Errors from the infrastructure. Generally each of these areas will involve different people so the challenge is designing a process that minimizes the time taken.	
To develop a variety of activities to accommodate for commonly occurring degrees of incidents, problems and known errors. For example, there are a wide variety of potential impacts that an incident, problem or known error may have on the environment. If we can categorize these impacts we can pre-build models for dealing with them.	
To establish ground rules that distinguish an Incident from a problem from a known error. An incident is seen as the symptom for larger or unknown issues that may exist in your environment.	

Develop working relationships with all other process areas. The Problem Management process is a proactive one requiring input from other process areas. Obvious links include Configuration Management (to verify configuration information and trends against configuration items) and Change Management (to check status of approved change progress that has been instigated to remove known errors). Problem Management will not be effective if there is not a clear understanding of the interface into the Incident Management process.	
Develop a sound Problem Management process and look for continuous improvement.	

Use these objectives to generate discussion about others that may be more appropriate to list than those provided.

Copyright The Art of Service │ Brisbane, Australia│ Email:service@theartofservice.com
Web: http://theartofservice.com │ eLearning: http://theartofservice.org │ Phone: +61 (0)7 3252 2055

6.3 *Policies, Objectives and Scope*

IT Services

Policies, Objectives and Scope
Process: Problem Management

Status:	In draft	
	Under Review	
	Sent for Approval	
	Approved	
	Rejected	
Version:	<<your version>>	
Release Date:		

Policies, Objectives and Scope for Problem Management

The document is not to be considered an extensive statement as its topics have to be generic enough to suit any reader for any organization. However, the reader will certainly be reminded of the key topics that have to be considered.

Policy Statement

A course of action, guiding principle, or procedure considered expedient, prudent, or advantageous

Use this text box to answer the "SENSE OF URGENCY" question regarding this process.

Why is effort being put into this process?
Not simply because someone thinks it's a good idea. That won't do. The reason has to be based in business benefits.

You must be able to concisely document the reason behind starting or improving this process.
Is it because of legal requirements or competitive advantage? Perhaps the business has suffered major problems or user satisfaction ratings are at the point where outsourcing is being considered.

A policy statement any bigger than this text box, may be too lengthy to read, lose the intended audience with detail, not be clearly focussed on answering the WHY question for this process.

The attached Policy Statement was;

Prepared by: _____

On: <<date>>

And accepted by: _____

On: <<date>>

Objectives Statement

Use this text box to answer the "WHERE ARE WE GOING" question regarding this process.

What will be the end result of this process and how will we know when we have reached the end result?
Will we know because we will establish a few key metrics or measurements or will it be a more subjective decision, based on instinct?

A generic sample statement on the "objective" for Problem Management is:
The Problem Management process aims to improve IT Service quality by providing an approach to investigate and analyse the underlying cause of the Incidents and Errors that occur in our IT Infrastructure. The actions to achieve this include the analysis of Incidents, Problems and Known Errors. The process must review achievements based on customer expectations and take steps to improve or modify the process accordingly.

Note the keywords in the statement. **For the statement on Problem Management they are "analyse the underlying cause" and "review achievements based on customer expectations". These are definite areas that we can set metrics for and therefore measure progress.**

An objective statement any bigger than this text box, may be too lengthy to read, lose the intended audience with detail, not be clearly focussed on answering the WHERE question for this process.

Something worked toward or striven for; a goal.

.Copyright The Art of Service | Brisbane, Australia | Email:service@theartofservice.com
Web: http://theartofservice.com | eLearning: http://theartofservice.org | Phone: +61 (0)7 3252 2055

The above Objective Statement was;

Prepared by: _____

On: <<date>>

And accepted by: _____

On: <<date>>

Scope Statement

The area covered by a given activity or subject

Use this text box to answer the "WHAT" question regarding this process.

What are the boundaries for this process?

What does the information flow look like into this process and from this process to other processes and functional areas?

A generic sample statement on the "scope" for Problem Management is:

The Problem Management process will be responsible for investigating the cause of all Priority 1 and 2 Incidents that have occurred on the following IT Services:

- **Email**
- **HR Applications**
- **Logistics Applications and Hardware**
- **Etc**

Problem Management will not be responsible for those components that exist under the banner of Applications Development and Project Management.

<< Important Note: The above scope provides some initial limits for this process. As the process matures the scope needs to be revisited to encompass a larger area, i.e. investigating the cause of **all** incidents >>

The attached Scope Statement was;

Prepared by: _____

On: <<date>>

And accepted by: _____

On: <<date>>

6.4 Business and IT Flyers

IT Services

Process: Problem Management

Business and IT Flyers

Status:	In draft	
	Under Review	
	Sent for Approval	
	Approved	
	Rejected	
Version:	<<your version>>	
Release Date:		

Introduction

The following pages provide 2 examples of flyers that can printed and distributed throughout your organization.

They are designed to be displayed in staff rooms.

Note, they are examples, and your input is required to complete the flyers.

Remember, the important thing is to ensure that the message delivered in the flyer is appropriate to the audience that will be reading it.

So think about how and where you will be distributing the flyers.

Problem Management

IT Services Department

Key Points:

- **Proactive Approach**

- **Removal of Known Errors.**

- **Fewer incidents**

- **Increased confidence**

- **<<other points>>**

<<Corporate Logo or image of choice>>

Wanted: Long Term Stability

The IT Department is embarking on a Problem Management implementation Program.

Problem Management is a set of activities designed to remove errors from the IT infrastructure.

<<First, determine the audience of this flyer. This could be anyone who might benefit from the information it contains, for example, IT employees or business staff.

The most exciting element of the program is the Proactive activities, designed to prevent errors even before they occur.

Traditionally our focus has been on fixing err as they occur. As of <<mm-yyyy>> that will change.

New processes will be in pla to head off potentially damaging, costly and time consuming errors in advanc

Provide contact lists for the Department as well as the business managers that the can contact.>>

Benefits
-List the benefits to the intended audience
-Keep it simple
-Use bullet points

Process Details
-Proactive activities
-Reactive activities

Contact Details
-List the contacts
-Add relevant graphics

Problem Management

IT SERVICE IMPROVEMENT PROGRAM

HELP US HELP YOU

Contact your immediate Manager to let them know
what you need to do your job better

INCREASED SERVICE AVAILABILITY THROUGH FEWER
PROBLEMS IS OUR GOAL

KNOW YOUR SERVICE RIGHTS

Sponsored by IT SERVICES

**"Constantly improving and aligning to your
needs"**

6.5 Email Text

IT Services

Process: Problem Management

Email Text

Status:	In draft	
	Under Review	
	Sent for Approval	
	Approved	
	Rejected	
Version:	<<your version>>	
Release Date:		

Introduction

In the next section of this document is an example email text that can be distributed across your organization.

Note, that this is just one piece of text for one email.

However, it is advisable to create a few different versions of the below text, which you can store in this document, for future use.

This is very important, as each time you send an email regarding your Problem Management process it should be different and targeted to the correct audience.

This document provides a method for also keeping track of your communication that you have made to the rest of the organization, and to keep in focus the promises that have been made regarding this process.

Dear << insert audience here, for example, Customer, IT Staff, Marketing Dept etc. >>

Problem Management

The IT Department <<give a specific name here if appropriate>> is embarking on a Problem Management implementation program.

What does this mean to you?

The IT Department continually strives to improve the service it delivers to its customers. The IT Services department provides internal support for <<e.g. Business applications and equipment: Enter any appropriate details here>>.

In order to improve the IT Services and ensure that they are aligned with the needs of the organization, we have decided to embark on a service improvement program. This program will result in the implementation of a process called Problem Management.

What is Problem Management?

This process is responsible for defining, recording, agreeing and improving IT Services. It is a process that is there to ensure that service quality is kept to a maximum.

We have defined the Goal for Problem Management as follows:

<< INSERT YOUR GOAL FOR PROBLEM MANAGEMENT HERE or use this one (or a variant of it). The goal for Problem Management is the PERMANENT removal of errors in the IT infrastructure. Such errors lead to issues for our end-users/customers in the form of an inability to use the IT Services for the purposes for which they were intended. It is for this reason and the growing importance of IT services in our organization that this program is one of importance.>>

What is your involvement?

The task of removing errors is ongoing and can take time to see results. In the short term we simply ask that you continue to contact the Service Desk/Help Desk/Local Support representative to report any issues you are facing with the IT services.

It is only with a continuing flow of data regarding issues that you are facing that we can take steps to identify and then remove these errors from the IT infrastructure that we manage.

We have appointed a Problem Manager to help drive this process. The Problem Manager will be the interface between the IT Department and the Department heads within the organization.

The Problem Manager is <<name>> and can be contact on <<phone/e-mail>>.

We will be making available a series of metrics/measurements regarding the process activities. These measurements are designed to help us demonstrate the overall benefits of implementing the program.

The following can be considered a list of benefits to be derived from the process:

<<

- List benefits applicable to your audience.
- For example: Benefits to the Business:
    - Smaller amounts of downtime due to IT errors
    - Ability to demonstrate best practice IT department
- For example: Benefits to the IT Department
    - Increased credibility with end users/customers
    - Reacting appropriately agreed levels of service

\>\>

The commencement date of the new process is scheduled for: <<
insert date >>

OR

Completion of the process will be: << insert date >>

This is a detailed process and there may be some operational
difficulties to overcome, but with your support, I am sure we can
provide an extremely beneficial process to both the Business /
<<organization name>> and IT.

If you have any questions regarding this, please do not hesitate to
contact me at << phone number >>

<< Your Name and Titles >>

6.6 Problem Category Definition

IT Services

Problem and Known Error:

Category Definitions

Status:	In draft	
	Under Review	
	Sent for Approval	
	Approved	
	Rejected	
Version:	<<your version>>	
Release Date:		

Document Control

Author

Prepared by <name and / or department>

Document Source

This document is located on the LAN under the path:

I:/IT Services/Service Support/Problem Management

Document Approval

This document has been approved for use by the following:

♦ <first name, last name>, IT Services Manager

♦ <first name, last name>, IT Service Delivery Manager

♦ <first name, last name>, National IT Help Desk Manager

Amendment History

Issue	Date	Amendments	Completed By

Distribution List

When this procedure is updated the following copyholders must be advised through email that an updated copy is available on the intranet site:

<Company Name> Business Unit	Stakeholders
IT	

Introduction

Purpose

The purpose of this document is to provide the IT Organisation with the specifications of the information to be captured on a Problem Ticket and Known Error Ticket.

Scope

This document describes the following:

- details of Problem and Known Error Ticket classifications

Audience

This document is relevant to all staff in <company name>

Ownership

IT Services has ownership of this document.

Related Documentation

Include in this section any related Problem Management reference numbers and other associated documentation:

- PROB6200 Problem Management Implementation Plan / Project Plan
- PROB6300 Problem Management Policies, Guidelines and Scope Document
- PROB6500 Problem Management Process

Executive Overview

Describe the purpose, scope and organization of the document.

Problem Management Overview

The documents intent is to provide definitions to be captured on Problem and Known Error tickets.

The definition of a Problem is:

The unknown underlying cause of one or more incidents or errors that have occurred or exist in the IT Infrastructure.

The definition of a Known Error is:

The cause of one or more incidents or problems have been identified and recorded as a Known Error.

Status Types

Each Problem and Known Error ticket should record the current status of that ticket. The following table lists some examples:

Value	Notes
New	Default status on ticket.
Contact	Customer has been contacted.
Notified	Used to initiate & record notification of ticket to 2nd line support or 3rd Parties.
Committed	Acceptance of call by support group.
Solving	Solving by support group.
Pending	This is a wait status
Resolved	Ticket is resolved
Closed	Ticket is closed, Customer / End User has confirmed service restoration.

It may also be necessary to break this down further and include a sub-status or a status reason that can be nested under each of the above status types. Some examples are illustrated in the following table:

Status Reason	Notes
Service Desk	The ticket is with the Service Desk for that status
Support Group	The ticket is with 2nd line support for that status
3rd Party	Stop SLA Clock
Canc. by Customer	
Canc. by IT Department	
Customer Action Needed	Stop SLA Clock
Customer Mgt	Stop SLA Clock
Customer Not Available	Stop SLA Clock
Customer Requested Delay	Stop SLA Clock
Customer Support Group	Stop SLA Clock
Down No Loan	
Down Waiting Loan	
Down Waiting Rep	
Down Waiting Spares	
Up Fixed & Monitoring	
Up Waiting Loan	
Up Waiting Repair	
Up Waiting Spares	
Up Waiting Test	

Definition Details

Problem and Known Error Categories

The problem and known error categories are high level definitions. Once you establish your categories, then it is important to provide a further break down.

For the purpose of Problem and Known Errors, these will break down into the following:

- ➢ Problem Tickets
  - o Categories
    - ▪ Subcategories
      - • Symptom Codes
- ➢ Known Errors
  - o Categories
    - ▪ Subcategories
      - • Cause Codes

The below table lists some examples of high level categories that are applicable for both Problem Tickets and Known Error Tickets:

Value	Notes
Backup and Recovery	
Batch Processing	
Communications	
Environment	
Hardware	
Software	
Performance	
Printing	
Security	
Unscheduled Outage	

Subcategory

Against the Categories listed above, some IT Service Management tools will allow further breakdown in the information. This is sometimes called a subcategory. The following list provides some examples:

- Business Applications
- Client Systems
- Network LAN
- Network WAN
- Shared Infrastructure
- Telecoms
- etc

Product Type

It is also possible to now add a third level ticket categorisation. This can be placed at the product type level. This information does not need to be nested, but can be made available regardless of the ticket type (i.e. problem or known error), Category and Subcategory.

The following list provides some examples for product types:

- PABX
- Phone
- Mobile Phone
- PDA
- Laptop
- Standard Application
- Non-Standard Application
- Desktop
- Printer
- Router
- Switch
- Consumable
- Etc.

Problem Ticket Symptom Codes

The following table provides a list of possible symptom codes to capture on your Problem Tickets:

Value	Notes
Abnormal O,S,V	
Damaged	
Degraded Operation	
Error Message	
Failures - No operation	
Jamming	
Malfunctioning	
Out of tolerance	
Preventative Maintenance due	
Poor Print Quality	
Safety hazard	
Unable receive data	
Certification Appears Due	

This is not an extensive list, but provides a good example of some of the symptom codes that may be required on a problem ticket

A good place to look for an extensive list of symptom codes would be your Incident Management process and Incident Tickets. End Users and Customers are very good at describing symptoms. If you are choosing to report this information then it would be a very good idea to use terms that the End Users and Customers are already familiar with.

Known Error Cause Codes

The following table provides a list of Cause Codes to be used on your Known Error Tickets.

Value	Notes
3rd Party Responsible	
Below revision	
Certification due	
Customer damage	
Failing assembly	
Faulty Spare Part	
Foreign object	
HW incompatibility	
Improper Lubrication	
Improper setup	
Incorrect application	
Incorrect Procedure Used	
Incorrect Process	
Known fault	
Mechanical part	
No fault found	
Not applicable	
Operational Procedure Fault	
Other	
Periodical Main Fault	
Restricted airflow	
Software error	
Training	
Training Reqd	
Withdrawn by <<company>>	
Withdrawn by customer	

Resolution Codes

The following table provides a list of resolution codes that can be used on either Problem Tickets or Known Error tickets. However, most will probably more applicable to the Known Error Tickets. For Known Error tickets, it will be most likely that a Change Request has been raised to remove the known error; therefore this value may not be applicable in most cases and can therefore be ignored.

Value	Notes
Adjustment carried out	
Calibration carried out	
Cancelled	
Change Request Raised	
Consumable replaced	
Customer advised	
Documentation	
Fix Not Viable	*Remember, sometimes it may cost more to fix than it does in loss of productivity.*
Foreign object removed	
Lubricated	
No fix available	
On site repair	

On site spare exchange	
On site unit exchange	
Operator error	
Phone fix	
PM carried out	
Rebooted	*This is more a workaround than a permanent solution.*
Referred to 3 party	
Reload software	
Reseated PCB	
Upgraded	
Withdrawn by operator	

Time and Materials

When undergoing an Error Assessment to understand the viability of removing the Known Error from the environment, a number of activities take place. For those who are mature in their processes, it may be necessary to record the amount of work carried out and the associated cost.

The below table provides some idea of time and material codes that could be captured on a Known Error ticket.

Value	Notes
Accommodation	
Administration	
Airfare	
Callout Fee	
Car Rental	
Change Management	
Consulting	
Desktop	
Service Desk	
Kilometres	
Labour	
Mainframe	
Midrange	
Network	
Onsite	
Operations	
Other	
Overtime	
Procurement	
Security	
Server	
Telephone	
Travel	
Value	
Voice	
Wait	

Appendices

Include any applicable appendixes that are needed.

Terminology

Make sure that all terminology is captured and documented correctly.

6.7 Known Error Ticket Template

IT Services

Known Error Ticket Template

Status:	In draft	
	Under Review	
	Sent for Approval	
	Approved	
	Rejected	
Version:	<<your version>>	
Release Date:		

Document Control

Author

Prepared by <name and / or department>

Document Source

This document is located on the LAN under the path:

I:/IT Services/Service Support/Known Error Management

Document Approval

This document has been approved for use by the following:

- <first name, last name>, IT Services Manager
- <first name, last name>, IT Service Delivery Manager
- <first name, last name>, National IT Help Desk Manager

Amendment History

Issue	Date	Amendments	Completed By

Distribution List

When this procedure is updated the following copyholders must be advised through email that an updated copy is available on the intranet site:

<Company Name> Business Unit	Stakeholders
IT	

Introduction

Purpose

The purpose of this document is to provide the IT Organisation with the specifications of information to be captured on a Known Error Ticket.

Scope

This document describes the following:

- details of Known Error Ticket attributes

Audience

This document is relevant to all staff in <company name>

Ownership

IT Services has ownership of this document.

Related Documentation

Include in this section any related Known Error Management reference numbers and other associated documentation:

- PROB6200 Problem Management Implementation Plan / Project Plan
- PROB6300 Problem Management Policies, Guidelines and Scope Document
- PROB6500 Problem Management Process
- PROB6700 Problem and Known Error Management Category Definition Document

Executive Overview

Describe the purpose, scope and organization of the document.

Known Error Management Overview

The document's intent is to provide a list of attributes / fields that need to be captured on a Known Error Ticket.

For the purpose of this document, a Known Error Ticket will be defined as a ticket to record information regarding an Error in the IT Infrastructure.

The definition of a Known Error is:

The known cause of one or more incidents or errors in the IT Infrastructure.

The document will guide you through several sections of information. These sections could be considered as different tabs on a ticket with in an ITSM tool.

The following definitions apply for the following tables:

> ➢ **Read Only:** No data may be entered into the field
> ➢ **System Generated:** The application will automatically generate the correct value(s).
> ➢ **Check Box:** A box, that when clicked upon will then show a mark, indicating that the box has been activated.

- ➢ **Linked Record:** Means that the field provides a button to allow the user to click on, which will take them to a list of records in the database, at which point they may choose a value to populate the field.
- ➢ **User Defined:** Field allows the user to enter any value that they wish
- ➢ **User Defined Array:** Field is considered a large text box which will allow the user to type multiple lines of text
- ➢ **Drop Box:** Field allows the user to click on a drop down list of information, where they are allowed to make one selection to populate the field.
- ➢ **Drop Box – Nested:** The values in this field are dependant on the values listed in the above Drop Box.
- ➢ **Break in Format:** Indicates where there will be a visual break in sets of information captured on the Known Error Ticket.

Ticket Details

This is a common set of information to be gathered for each Known Error Ticket.

Field	Description (Where Necessary)	Type of Field
Ticket ID	This is the number for the ticket. This should be an incremental number.	Read Only. System Generated.
Lead Owner	This is the person responsible for conducting the assessment of the Known Error.	Linked Record.

.Copyright The Art of Service │ Brisbane, Australia │ Email:service@theartofservice.com
Web: http://theartofservice.com │ eLearning: http://theartofservice.org │ Phone: +61 (0)7 3252 2055

Field	Description (Where Necessary)	Type of Field
First Name	Self Explanatory.	Read Only. Populated by Contact Name.
Last Name	Self Explanatory.	Read Only. Populated by Contact Name.
Employee Id.	It may be necessary to have a unique ID for each contact on the ticket. An employee id is common solution.	Read Only. Populated by Contact Name.
Email	Self Explanatory.	Read Only. Populated by Contact Name.
Phone #	Phone Number	Read Only. Populated by Contact Name.
Ext #	Extension Number	Read Only. Populated by Contact Name.
Fax #	Facsimile Number	Read Only. Populated by Contact Name.
Break in Format		
Location	This field should be a linked record and not reliant on the above information. The simple reason is that some employees in your organisation may move around and therefore their usual location may not be applicable.	Linked Record.
Room / Floor Ref.	Self Explanatory	Read Only. Populated by Location.
Cost Centre	Self Explanatory	Read Only. Populated by Location.

Field	Description (Where Necessary)	Type of Field
Break in Format		
Status	The status of the ticket. This will be initially set to open when first logged. Please see PROB6700 Problem and Known Error Category Definition Document for further information.	Drop Box.
Owner	Initially populated by the individual (operator) logging the ticket, however, this is a changeable field as tickets may change ownership due to various reasons. The owner of the ticket can only be a Service Desk representative.	Linked Record.
Category	Please see PROB6700 Problem and Known Error Category Definition Document for further information.	Drop Box
Subcategory	Please see PROB6700 Problem and Known Error Category Definition Document for further information.	Drop Box – Nested
Product Type	Please see PROB6700 Problem and Known Error Category Definition Document for further information.	Drop Box
Problem Type	Please see PROB6700 Problem and Known Error Category Definition Document for further information.	Drop Box - Nested
Impact	The impact is the measure of business criticality.	Drop Box
Urgency	Urgency is about the necessary speed to solve the ticket	Drop Box
Priority	Priority is defined by expected effort in resolving the ticket.	Drop Box
Break in Format		
Configuration Id.	The Configuration Item that appears to be involved with Error.	Linked Record
Type	The type of Configuration Item. For example: Hardware, Software, Printer, PC etc.	Read Only. Populated by Configuration Id.

Field	Description (Where Necessary)	Type of Field
Model	The model of the Configuration Item. For example: HP LaserJet, HP Desktop, Dell Desktop etc.	Read Only. Populated by Configuration Id.
Break in Format		
Assignment Group	The 2nd or 3rd Line Support group to which the ticket has been assigned.	Linked Record.
Assignee Name	An individual within the assignment group that is working on the ticket.	Linked Record.
Phone #	Self Explanatory	Read Only. Populated by the Assignee Name field.

Update Details

This section allows user input to capture all the work being carried out during the assessment of the Known Error.

Field	Description (Where Necessary)	Type of Field
Cause Code	The actual cause of the Error.	Drop Box.
Brief Description	A brief description of the ticket.	User Defined.
Description	A full description of the ticket.	User Defined Array.
Break in Format		
Ticket Update	Field to allow the users to type any updates.	User Defined Array.
Update History	Field that shows all previous entered updates.	Read Only.

Root Cause

This section allows input to capture information about the actual root cause of the Error. In some instances, it will not be possible to discover the root cause of a Problem.

Field	Description (Where Necessary)	Type of Field
Root Cause	A description of the actual root cause for the Known Error.	User Defined Array.
Work Around	A detailed description of any applicable work around that can be used to ensure the service can be restored as quickly as possible.	User Defined Array.

Assessment

Just because an Error may be found in the IT Infrastructure, there does not need to be an automatic assumption that it has to be removed. There needs to be an investigative period where the IT Organisation looks at the ramifications of removing the error, the associated cost of the error in the infrastructure, the cost for removing the error and the business requirements with regards to the removing the error.

This section provides a list of details that need to be captured during the assessment.

Field	Description (Where Necessary)	Type of Field
Business Impact Analysis	A full description of the impact of the error on the business.	User Defined Array.
Business Productivity Loss	An estimate on the Business Productivity Loss. For example: Very High, High, Medium, Low	Drop Box.
IT Productivity Loss	An estimate on the IT Productivity Loss resulting from Incidents occurring due to this error. For example: Very High, High, Medium, Low	Drop Box.
Removal Cost	As estimate on the cost to remove the Error from the infrastructure.	User Defined.

Technical Resources	A description of the technical skills required to remove the error from the infrastructure.	User Defined Array.
Required Configuration Items	A list of the Configuration Items required in the removal of the Error from the infrastructure.	Linked Record.
Planned Start Date	Planned Start date for the removal of the Error.	Date / Time field.
Planned End Date	Planned End date for having removed the Error.	Data / Time field.
Duration	Expected Duration to remove the Error.	User Defined.

Resolution Details

Field	Description (Where Necessary)	Type of Field
Resolution Code	The resolution code for the ticket. This may include values such as: Error Removed with RFC, Error Remains – Too Costly, Error Remains – Technically Impossible etc.	Drop Box.
Resolution Description	A brief description of the resolution given.	User Defined.
Resolution Details	A full description of the resolution applied to the ticket.	User Defined Array.

Related Tickets Details

It should be a function of the IT Service Management tool to allow users to associate other tickets to the Known Error Ticket being worked on.

The association would be done by a corresponding search and attachment process. This will be determined by the tool itself. When associating another ticket to the Known Error ticket, the following information will automatically be attached.

Field	Description (Where Necessary)	Type of Field
Incident Tickets		
Incident ID.	See document INC8800 Incident Ticket Template.	Read Only. Auto Populated.
Open Time	See document INC8800 Incident Ticket Template.	Read Only. Auto Populated.
Status	See document INC8800 Incident Ticket Template.	Read Only. Auto Populated.
Type	See document INC8800 Incident Ticket Template.	Read Only. Auto Populated.
Category	See document INC8800 Incident Ticket Template.	Read Only. Auto Populated.
Brief Description	See document INC8800 Incident Ticket Template.	Read Only. Auto Populated.
Problem Tickets		
Problem ID	See document PROB6800 Problem Ticket Template	Read Only. Auto Populated.
Open Time	See document PROB6800 Problem Ticket Template	Read Only. Auto Populated.
Status	See document PROB6800 Problem Ticket Template	Read Only. Auto Populated.

Field	Description (Where Necessary)	Type of Field
Category	See document PROB6800 Problem Ticket Template	Read Only. Auto Populated.
Brief Description	See document PROB6800 Problem Ticket Template	Read Only. Auto Populated.
Known Error Tickets		
Error ID	The ticket number for the Known Error Ticket.	Read Only. Auto Populated.
Open Time	The time that the Known Error Ticket was opened.	Read Only. Auto Populated.
Status	The current status of the Known Error Ticket.	Read Only. Auto Populated.
Category	The Category for the Known Error Ticket. Please see PROB6700 Problem and Known Error Category Definition Document	Read Only. Auto Populated.
Brief Description	A brief description for the Known Error Ticket.	Read Only. Auto Populated.
Request For Changes		
Change Number	See document CHG7800 Request for Change (RFC) Template.	Read Only. Auto Populated.
Category	See document CHG7800 Request for Change (RFC) Template.	Read Only. Auto Populated.
Phase	See document CHG7800 Request for Change (RFC) Template.	Read Only. Auto Populated.
Asset	See document CHG7800 Request for Change (RFC) Template.	Read Only. Auto Populated.
Description	See document CHG7800 Request for Change (RFC) Template.	Read Only. Auto Populated.

Field	Description (Where Necessary)	Type of Field
Planned Start Date	See document CHG7800 Request for Change (RFC) Template.	Read Only. Auto Populated.
Planned End Date	See document CHG7800 Request for Change (RFC) Template.	Read Only. Auto Populated.

History

Field	Description (Where Necessary)	Type of Field
Opened By	Name of the individual who opened / created / logged the ticket.	Linked Record.
Opened At	Time the ticket was opened / created / logged.	Date / Time Field.
Updated By	Name of the individual who updated the ticket	Linked Record.
Update At	Time the ticket was last updated.	Date / Time Field.
Resolved By	Name of the individual who placed the ticket into a resolved status.	Linked Record.
Resolved At	Time the ticket was resolved.	Date / Time Field.
Closed By	Name of the individual who closed the ticket.	Linked Record.
Closed At	Time the ticket was closed.	Date / Time Field.
Reopened By	Name of the individual who reopened the ticket.	Linked Record.
Reopened At	Time the ticket was reopened.	Date / Time Field.

Appendices

Include any applicable appendixes that are needed.

Terminology

Make sure that all terminology is captured and documented correctly.

IT Services

Reports and KPI Targets

Process: Problem Management

Status:	
Version:	0.1
Release Date:	

Reports and KPI Targets for Problem Management

The document is not to be considered an extensive statement as its topics have to be generic enough to suit any reader for any organization. However, the reader will certainly be reminded of the key topics that have to be considered.

This document serves as a GUIDE ON SUITABLE KEY PERFORMANCE INDICATORS (KPIs) and REPORTS FOR MANAGEMENT for the Problem Management process. This document provides a basis for completion within your own organization.

This document contains suggestions regarding the measures that would be meaningful for this process. The metrics demonstrated are intended to show the reader the range of metrics that can be used. The message must also be clear that technology metrics must be heavily supplemented with non-technical and business focused metrics/KPIs/measures.

This document was;

Prepared by: _____

On: <<date>>

And accepted by: _____

On: <<date>>

.Copyright The Art of Service │ Brisbane, Australia │ Email:service@theartofservice.com
Web: http://theartofservice.com │ eLearning: http://theartofservice.org │ Phone: +61 (0)7 3252 2055

Key performance indicators (KPIs)

Continuous improvement requires that each process needs to have a plan about "how" and "when" to measure its own performance. While there can be no set guidelines presented for the timing/when of these reviews; the "how" question can be answered with metrics and measurements.

With regard to timing of reviews then factors such as resource availability, cost and "nuisance factor" need to be accounted for. Many initiatives begin with good intentions to do regular reviews, but these fall away very rapidly. This is why the process owner must have the conviction to follow through on assessments and meetings and reviews, etc. If the process manager feels that reviews are too seldom or too often then the schedule should be changed to reflect that.

Establishing SMART targets is a key part of good process management.

SMART is an acronym for:

> **S**imple
>
> **M**easurable
>
> **A**chievable
>
> **R**ealistic
>
> **T**ime Driven

Metrics help to ensure that the process in question is running effectively.

With regard to PROBLEM MANAGEMENT the following metrics and associated targets should be considered:

Key Performance Indicator	Target Value (some examples)	Time Frame/Notes/Who
Using data from the Configuration Management Database (CMDB) indicate any particular Configuration items that are experiencing a large number or incidents, problems or known errors. **(for more information on the CMDB refer to the Configuration Management process at www.theartofservice.com CONFIGMGT).**		
Number of Problems raised Number of Problems identified as Known Errors Number of Known Errors that can be removed Number of Known Errors that have been removed		
Number of Problems and Known Errors identified due to proactive activities.		
Incident count related to problems and known errors made in previous period.		

.Copyright The Art of Service │ Brisbane, Australia │ Email:service@theartofservice.com
Web: http://theartofservice.com │ eLearning: http://theartofservice.org │ Phone: +61 (0)7 3252 2055

Number of Major Problem reviews completed.		
Others		

Special Tip: Beware of using percentages in too many cases. It may even be better to use absolute values when the potential number of maximum failures is less than 100.

Reports for Management

Management reports help identify future trends and allow review of the "health" of the process. Setting a security level on certain reports may be appropriate as may be categorizing the report as Strategic, Operational or Tactical.

The acid test for a relevant report is to have a sound answer to the question; "What decisions is this report helping management to make?" Management reports for Problem Management should include:

Report	Time Frame/Notes/Who
The number of Problems and Known Errors lodged, quantity rejected and the percentage that were issued as major impacts.	
Summary of problems that are still to be investigated. Management will be interested to see the number of higher priority problems still awaiting investigation. Importantly each outstanding problem should show how long it has been in this status. Problems that have been in waiting for long periods of time may be downgraded or even scrapped.	
Summary of Known Errors that are still to be assessed. Management will be interested in seeing the number of Known Errors and the costs in removing them.	
Backlog details of process activities work outstanding (along with potential negative impact regarding failure to complete the work in a timely manner) – but also provide solutions on how the backlog can be cleared.	

The number of problem and known errors attributable to different business areas is also useful. This will help Management to understand departments that are in a state of threat. Problems and Known Errors can indicate poor management, fluctuating internal or increasing pressures from external forces.	
Analysis and results of meetings completed	
The situation regarding the process staffing levels and any suggestions regarding redistribution, recruitment and training required.	
Human resource reporting including hours worked against project/activity (including weekend/after hours work).	
Audit Reports should verify that any selected Problem or Known Error contains all relevant and expected information. The audit will also review Proactive Problem meeting minutes and report any anomalies (for example action items not followed up on, scheduled Problem Management process reviews that didn't go ahead).	
Relevant Financial information– to be provided in conjunction with Financial Management for IT Services **(FINANCIALMGT).** This information will include a cost per change summary.	

6.9 *Communication Plan*

IT Services

Communication Plan
Process: Problem Management

Status:	In draft	
	Under Review	
	Sent for Approval	
	Approved	
	Rejected	
Version:	<<your version>>	
Release Date:		

Communication Plan for Problem Management

The document is not to be considered an extensive statement as its topics have to be generic enough to suit any reader for any organization. However, the reader will certainly be reminded of the key topics that have to be considered.

This document serves as a GUIDE FOR COMMUNICATIONS REQUIRED for the Problem Management process. This document provides a basis for completion within your own organization.

This document contains suggestions regarding information to share with others. The document is deliberately concise and broken into communication modules. This will allow the reader to pick and choose information for e-mails, flyers, etc. from one or more modules if and when appropriate.

This document was;

Prepared by: _____

On: <<date>>

And accepted by: _____

On: <<date>>

Initial Communication

Sell the Benefits.

First steps in communication require the need to answer the question that most people (quite rightly) ask when the IT department suggests a new system, a new way of working. WHY?

It is here that we need to promote and sell the benefits. However, be cautious of using generic words. Cite specific examples from your own organization that the reader will be able to relate to (to help develop specific examples contact service@theartofservice.com for competitive quotation).

Generic Benefit statements	Specific Organizational example
Improved IT Service Quality	This is important because…
Reduction in the number of Incidents	In recent times our incidents within IT have…
Provides Permanent Solutions	Apart from the obvious benefits, the IT department in recent times has…
Improved Organisational learning	A recent example of … saw the individual and others in the company start to…

The attached Communication module (or elements of) was/were distributed;

To: _____

On: <<date>>

By: _____

On: <<date>>

Problem Management Goal

The Goal of Problem Management.

The Goal of Problem Management can be promoted in the following manner.

<u>**Official Goal Statement**</u>**: Through a series of standardized and repeatable activities, the IT Department will reduce the number of Incidents that occur and minimize any adverse impacts on the Business and the IT Infrastructure.**

- High visibility and wide channels of communication are essential in this process. Gather specific Problem and Known Error Requirements from nominated personnel

(Special Tip: Beware of using only Managers to gain information from, as the resistance factor will be high)

Oversee the monitoring of process to ensure that the business needs of IT are not impacted, but taking into account that changes are required to ensure continued high levels of IT Service Delivery and Support.

Provide relevant reports to nominated personnel.

(Special Tip: Beware of reporting only to Managers. If you speak to a lot of people regarding Service Support and Delivery then you need to establish ways to report to these people the outcomes and progress of the discussions).

Copyright The Art of Service | Brisbane, Australia | Email:service@theartofservice.com
Web: http://theartofservice.com | eLearning: http://theartofservice.org | Phone: +61 (0)7 3252 2055

The attached Problem Management Goals module was distributed;

To: _____

On: <<date>>

By: _____

On: <<date>>

Problem Management Activities

Intrusive & Hidden Activities

The list of actions in this module will have a direct impact on end users and IT Staff. They will be curious as to why staff are working with them in this manner, rather than the historical method of just "doing it". There could be an element of suspicion and resistance, so consider different strategies to overcome this initial scepticism.

Problem Control

- Set out clear procedures to record and track Problems.
- Make a clear distinction between an Incident, Problem and Known Error
- Provide a clear method for recording and distributing work around solutions back to the Service Desk and End Users alike.
- Provide a clear and concise method for classifying Problems
- It is important to ensure that proper reporting is established for both the Business and IT.

Error Control

- Set out clear procedures and control in identifying errors and how to record them in your environment.
- An important aspect of error control is the error assessment activity. In this activity we have very clear communication responsibilities. The error assessment will let IT know if it is viable or desirable to remove the error from the IT infrastructure. To make this decision we need clear information form the business regarding loss of productivity that occurs from the incidents that result from this error. Business involvement and communication is essential.
- Provide a clear method for recording the resolution of the Error and any associated work around.
- Communicate how this activity also relates to the process of Change Management

Proactive Problem Management

- This activity aims at identifying and resolving Problems before any Incidents can occur. To be able to do this successfully, there is a strong reliance on information from other processes, especially Availability Management
- Establish clear methods in recording and identifying trends that occur in the IT Infrastructure
- The trend analysis should provide the IT organisation the ability to pin point areas in their IT Infrastructure so as to perform targeted preventative action.
- This activity is also involved in providing information to the IT organisation and the business as well. This information should provide insight into the effort and resources needed to investigate and diagnose problems and known errors.
- Only through proper meaningful measurements can management determine the effectiveness of this process.

Information regarding activities was distributed;

To: _____

On: <<date>>

By: _____

On: <<date>>

Problem Management Planning

Costs

Information relating to costs may be a topic that would be held back from general communication. Failure to convince people of the benefits will mean total rejection of associated costs. If required, costs fall under several categories:

- Personnel – audit verification staff, database management team (Set-up and ongoing)
- Accommodation – Physical location (Set-up and ongoing)
- Software – Tools (Set-up and ongoing)
- Hardware – Infrastructure (Set-up)
- Education – Training (Set-up and ongoing)
- Procedures – external consultants etc (Set-up)

The costs of implementing Problem Management will be outweighed by the benefits. For example, many organizations have a negative perception of the incident management process as it doesn't remove the cause. Users are constantly complaining that the issue they had today was the same one yesterday. Problem Management will remove this perception, reduce the reactiveness of the IT Organisation and by default will start providing better IT Services.

A well run Problem Management process will make major inroads into altering the perception of the IT Organisation.

Details regarding the cost of Problem Management were distributed;

To: _____

On: <<date>>

By: _____

On: <<date>>

IT Services

Roles, Responsibilities

Process: Problem Management

Status:	In draft	
	Under Review	
	Sent for Approval	
	Approved	
	Rejected	
Version:	<<your version>>	
Release Date:		

Detailed responsibilities of the Problem Management process owner.

The Problem Manager:

	Description	Notes/Comments
1.	Will develop and maintain the Problem Control Process. Will develop and maintain the Error Control Process. Will develop and maintain the Proactive Problem Management Process.	*Use the notes/Comments column in different ways. If you are looking to apply for a process role, then you can check yourself against the list (with ticks or look to update your resume).*
2.	Will coordinate process reviews utilizing independent parties to provide an objective view on the simplicity of the process and areas for improvement. Will be responsible for implementing any design improvements identified.	
3.	Conducts reviews on Problem and Known Errors that have been identified and actioned to verify that all steps were completed and the objective of the process was achieved.	*If you are looking to appoint a process manager or promote someone from within the organization you can make notes about their abilities in the particular area.*
4.	Arrange and run all Proactive Problem Management reviews with the problem team. This will be done in conjunction with the Service Level Management process and the Service Improvement Plan. This will also involve the Technical Observation Post that would have been set up by Availability Management.	

5.	The Problem Manager will liaise with the relevant parties involved during the preventative targeting activity to ensure activities are co-ordinated and carried out according to plan.	
6.	Will control and review: ➢ Any outstanding process related actions ➢ Current targets for service performance ➢ The process mission statement	
7.	Make available relevant, concise reports that are both timely and readable for Customers and Management	

Detailed skills of the Problem Management process owner.

The Problem Manager:

	Description	Notes/Comments
1.	The Problem Manager will display a communication style based around negotiation and information.	*Use the notes/Comments column in different ways. If you are looking to apply for a process role, then you can check yourself against the list (with ticks or look to update your resume).*
2.	High degree of analytical skills to be able to assess the impact of problems and known errors on different business systems and people.	
3.	Semi-Technical ability in being able to read data from the Configuration Management process that will help with the identification of potentially affected items involved in a problem or known error.	

4.	An ability to run a meeting according to strict guidelines (not to get side-tracked on items that one person may be interested in).	*If you are looking to appoint a process manager or promote someone from within the organization you can make notes about their abilities in the particular area.*
5.	The Problem Manager must be able to communicate with people at all levels of the organization. This is especially important during meetings.	
6.	The process manager must be able to demonstrate ways to "do things differently" that will improve the process.	
7.	Must be able to think logically about potential problems and known errors that could affect the organization and design appropriate assessment and diagnosis activities.	

6.11 Implementation and Project Plan

IT Services

Implementation Plan/Project Plan
Skeleton Outline

Process: Problem Management

Status:	In draft	
	Under Review	
	Sent for Approval	
	Approved	
	Rejected	
Version:	<<your version>>	
Release Date:		

Planning and implementation for Problem Management

This document as described provides guidance for the planning and implementation of the Problem Management ITIL process.

The document is not to be considered an extensive plan as its topics have to be generic enough to suit any reader for any organization. However, the reader will certainly be reminded of the key topics that have to be considered for planning and implementation of this process.

Initial planning

When beginning the process planning the following items must be completed:

CHECK ☺☺☹ or ✓✗ or date	DESCRIPTION
	Get agreement on the objective (use the ITIL definition), purpose, scope, and implementation approach (e.g. Internal, outsourced, hybrid) for the process.
	Assign a person to the key role of process manager/owner. This person is responsible for the process and all associated systems.
	Conduct a review of activities that would currently be considered as an activity associated with this process. Make notes and discuss the "re-usability" of that activity.

	Create and gain agreement on a high-level process plan and a design for any associated process systems. NOTE: the plan need not be detailed. Too many initiatives get caught up in too much detail in the planning phase. **KEEP THE MOMENTUM GOING.**
	Review the finances required for the process as a whole and any associated systems (expenditure including people, software, hardware, accommodation). Don't forget that the initial expenditure may be higher than the ongoing costs. Don't forget annual allowances for systems maintenance or customizations to systems by development staff.
	Agree to the policy regarding this process

Create Strategic statements.

Policy Statement

The policy establishes the "<u>SENSE OF URGENCY</u>" for the process.

It helps us to think clearly about and agree on the reasons WHY effort is put into this process.

An inability to answer this seemingly simple, but actually complex question is a major stepping stone towards successful implementation

The most common mistake made is that reasons regarding IT are given as the WHY we should do this. Reasons like *"to make our IT department more efficient"* are far too generic and don't focus on the real issue behind why this process is needed.

The statement must leave the reader in no doubt that the benefits of this process will be far reaching and contribute to the business in a clearly recognizable way.

.Copyright The Art of Service │ Brisbane, Australia│ Email:service@theartofservice.com
Web: http://theartofservice.com │ eLearning: http://theartofservice.org │ Phone: +61 (0)7 3252 2055

Objective Statement

When you are describing the end or ultimate goal for a unit of activity that is about to be undertaken you are outlining the OBJECTIVE for that unit of activity.

Of course the activity may be some actions for just you or a team of people. In either case, writing down the answer to WHERE will this activity lead to me/us/the organization is a powerful exercise.

There are many studies that indicate the simple act of putting a statement about the end result expected onto a piece of paper, then continually referring to it, makes achieving that end result realistic.

As a tip regarding the development of an objective statement; don't get caught up in spending hours on this. Do it quickly and go with your instincts or first thoughts – BUT THEN, wait a few days and review what you did for another short period of time and THEN commit to the outcome of the second review as your statement.

Scope Statement

In defining the scope of this process we are answering what activities and what "information interfaces" does this process have.

Do not get caught up in trying to be too detailed about the information flow into and out of this process. What is important is that others realize that information does in fact flow.

For example, with regard to the PROBLEM MANAGEMENT process we can create a simple table such as:

Problem Management Information flows

Process		Process	Information
Problem Management	to	Incident Management	Known Error records, work arounds, problem resolutions for incident tickets
Incident Management	to	Problem Management	Logged incidents against CIs that may have an underlying cause.
Problem Management	to	Change Management	Requests For Change to remove a known error from the IT Infrastructure
Change Management	to	Problem Management	Participation in the Post Implementation Review
Problem Management	to	Availability Management	Reports of availability related problems and known errors
Availability Management	to	Problem Management	Availability reports used to indicate current or future problems or known errors

Steps for Implementation.

There can be a variety of ways to implement this process. For a lot of organizations a staged implementation may be suitable. For others a "big bang" implementation – due to absolute equality may be appropriate.

In reality however, we usually look at implementation according to pre-defined priorities. Consider the following **options** and then apply a suitable model to your own organization or case study.

STEPS	NOTES/ /RELEVANCE/DATES/ WHO
Define the Objective and Scope for Problem Management	
Establish and agree on a clear definition for the words "Problem" and "Known Error" within the context of the process.	
Seek initial approval	
Establish and Define Roles and Responsibilities for the process. Appoint a Problem Manager.	
Establish and Define Problem Categories and Known Error Categories	
Establish Problem Management Process	
Establish and Define Relationship with Incident Management, Change Management and Availability Management	
Establish monitoring levels	
Define reporting standards	
Publicize and market	

The priority selection has to be made with other factors in mind, such as competitive analysis, any legal requirements, and desires of "politically powerful influencers".

Costs

The cost of process implementation is something that must be considered before, during and after the implementation initiative. The following points and table help to frame these considerations:

(A variety of symbols have been provided to help you indicate required expenditure, rising or falling expenditure, level of satisfaction regarding costs in a particular area, etc.)

	Initial	During	Ongoing
Personnel Costs of people for initial design of process, implementation and ongoing support	✓	◀	▸
Accommodation Costs of housing new staff and any associated new equipment and space for documents or process related concepts.	☺	☺	☹
Software New tools required to support the process and/or the costs of migration from an existing tool or system to the new one. Maintenance costs			
Hardware New hardware required to support the process activities. IT hardware and even new desks for staff.			
Education Re-education of existing staff to learn new techniques and/or learn to operate new systems.			
Procedures Development costs associated with filling in the detail of a process activity. The step-by-step recipe guides for all involved and even indirectly involved personnel.			

In most cases, costs for Process implementation have to be budgeted for (or allocated) well in advance of expenditure. Part of this step involves deciding on a charging mechanism (if any) for the new services to be offered.

Build the team

Each process requires a process owner and in most situations a team of people to assist.

The Problem Management process is one of the processes in the Service Support set that shows very visible benefits from the outset.

Of course a lot will be dependent on the timing of the implementation and whether it is to be staged or implemented as one exercise.

Analyse current situation and FLAG

Naturally there are many organizations that have many existing procedures/processes and people in place that feel that the activities of Problem Management is already being done. It is critical to identify these systems and consider their future role as part of the new process definition.

Examples of areas to review are:

Area	Notes
Power teams	
Current formal procedures	
Current informal procedures	
Current role descriptions	
Existing organizational structure	
Spreadsheets, databases and other repositories	
Other…	

Implementation Planning

After base decisions regarding the scope of the process and the overall planning activities are complete we need to address the actual implementation of the process.

It is unlikely that there will not be some current activity or work being performed that would fit under the banner of this process. However, we can provide a comprehensive checklist of points that must be reviewed and done.

Implementation activities for Problem Management

Activity	Notes/Comments/Time Frame/Who
Review current and existing Problem Management practices in greater detail. Make sure you also review current process connections from these practices to other areas of IT Service Delivery and Support.	
Review the ability of existing functions and staff. Can we "reuse" some of the skills to minimize training, education and time required for implementation?	
Establish the accuracy and relevance of current processes, procedures and meetings. As part of this step if any information is credible document the transition from the current format to any new format that is selected.	
Decide how best to select any vendor that will provide assistance in this process area (including tools, external consultancy or assistance to help with initial high workload during process implementation).	
Establish a selection guideline for the evaluation and selection of tools required to support this process area (i.e. Problem Management tools).	

Purchase and install tools required to support this process (i.e. Problem Management tool). Ensure adequate skills transfer and on-going support is catered for if external systems are selected.	
Create any required business processes interfaces for this process that can be provided by the automated tools (e.g. reporting – frequency, content).	
Document and get agreement on roles, responsibilities and training plans.	
Communicate with and provide necessary education and training for staff that covers the actual importance of the process and the intricacies of being part of the process itself.	

An important point to remember is that if this process is to be implemented at the same time as other processes that it is crucial that both implementation plans and importantly timing of work is complementary.

Cutover to new processes

The question of when a new process actually starts is one that is not easy to answer. Most process activity evolves without rigid starting dates and this is what we mean when we answer a question with "that's just the way it's done around here".

Ultimately we do want the new process to become the way things are done around here, so it may even be best not to set specific launch dates, as this will set the expectation that from the given date all issues relating to the process will disappear (not a realistic expectation).

7 IT Service Management (ITSM) Capability Assessment

Based on ITIL® Version 3

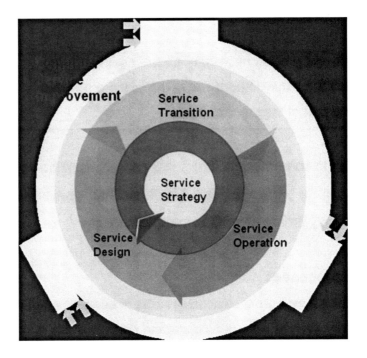

Service Operation Questionnaire

7.1 Introduction

This document is one part of a broader assessment model enabling you to establish the extent to which your organization has adopted the good practice guidance for IT Service Management (ITSM) based on the Information Technology Infrastructure Library (ITIL) version 3.

The assessment scheme is composed of a simple questionnaire which enables you to ascertain which areas should be addressed next in order to improve the overall quality and performance of ITIL processes. The assessment is based on the generic capability levels defined by the Capability Maturity Model Integrated (CMMI) framework, which recognizes that there are a number of characteristics which need to be in place for effective process management. In general, CMMI provides guidance for efficient, effective improvement across multiple process disciplines in an organization.

To establish where a particular organization stands in relation to the process capability framework, a variable number of questions should be answered. The questions are weighted, i.e. those which are deemed as having a slightly higher significance are considered mandatory for a 'Yes' answer at each level of capability. These questions are denoted by a 'M' symbol in the 'No' column, (indicating that a 'Yes' answer is required if the level is to be achieved).

The assessment is used to establish a baseline of current practices in the organization and to assist in the development of improvement initiatives for processes that can be used when they:

- Decide what services they should be providing, define standard services, and let people know about them
- Make sure they have everything they need to deliver a service, including people, processes, consumables, and equipment
- Get new systems in place, change existing systems, retire obsolete systems, all while making sure disruption to existing services and customers is minimized

131

- Set up agreements, take care of service requests, and operate services
- Make sure they have the resources needed to deliver services and that services are available when needed—at an appropriate cost
- Handle what goes wrong—and prevent it from going wrong in the first place if possible
- Ensure they are ready to recover from potential disasters and get back to delivering services if the disaster occurs

Although it is conceptually feasible to improve all processes, it is not economical to improve all processes to level 5. Therefore the results of the capability assessment should be analyzed in conjunction with the defined business objectives and stakeholders' priorities for improvement.

Scoring model for assessing process capability

There are five levels defined within the CMMI framework, as predictability, effectiveness and control of an organization's processes are believed to improve as the organization moves up these five levels.

Capability Level	General characteristics
Level 0 – Non-existent	Investigation shows no existing process goals and an effective lacking of process activities being employed.
Level 1 – Performed (Ad-hoc)	Processes at this level are typically undocumented and in a state of dynamic change, tending to be driven in an ad hoc, uncontrolled and reactive manner by users or events. This provides a chaotic or unstable environment for the processes. In general, the process supports and enables the work needed to provide Services, but improvements may be lost over time.

Level 2 - Managed	A managed process is a performed (capability level 1) process that has the basic infrastructure in place to support the process. It is planned and executed in accordance with policy; employs skilled people who have adequate resources to produce controlled outputs; involves relevant stakeholders; is monitored, controlled, and reviewed; and is evaluated for adherence to its process description. The process discipline reflected by capability level 2 helps to ensure that existing practices are retained during times of stress. There may be a high reliance on individual skill level due to inconsistent documentation or training made available.

Level 3 – Defined	A defined process is a managed (capability level 2) process that is tailored to be effective under various environmental conditions and with a range of appropriate inputs.
	At capability level 3, the standards, process descriptions, and procedures for a project are tailored from the organization's set of standard processes to suit a particular project or organizational unit and therefore are more consistent, except for the differences allowed by the tailoring guidelines.
	At capability level 3, processes are managed more proactively using an understanding of the interrelationships of the process activities and detailed measures of the process and its work products.
Level 4 - Quantitatively Managed	A quantitatively managed process is a defined (capability level 3) process that is controlled using statistical and other quantitative techniques. Quantitative objectives for quality and process performance are established and used as criteria in managing the process. Quality and process performance is understood in statistical terms and is managed throughout the life of the process.

Level 5 – Optimizing	An optimizing process is a quantitatively managed (capability level 4) process that is improved based on an understanding of the common causes of variation inherent in the process. The focus of an optimizing process is on continually improving the range of process performance through both incremental and innovative improvements.

Directions for conducting assessment

Follow these steps to ascertain the organizational capability level for a specific ITSM process:

- Start at Level 1 and answer each question, ticking 'Y' or 'N' column as appropriate;

- Check the level criteria given at the foot of the table of Level 1 questions. If the criteria for Level 1 are satisfied, move on to the next level;

- Continue up the levels until the criteria for the current level are not entirely met. For example, should the criteria be satisfied for Levels 1, 2, 3, but are not quite met for Level 4, then no further questions need be attempted and the organization's capability level is deemed to be 3.

7.2 Service Operation Overview

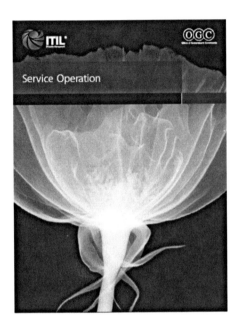

The Service Operation lifecycle phase is primarily focused on the management of IT Services that ensures effectiveness and efficiency in delivery and support.

Successful Service Operation requires coordination and execution of the activities and processes required to deliver and manage services at agreed levels to business users and customers. Service Operation is also responsible for ongoing management of the technology that is used to deliver and support services.

One of Service Operation's key roles is dealing with the conflict between maintaining the status quo, adapting to the changing business and technological environments and achieving a balance between conflicting sets of priorities.

As the centre point for the majority of activity in an IT organization, Service Operation will be faced with many challenges in achieving a balance between all varying objectives defined and perspectives that are required.

Perspectives that are considered include:

- Technology – focusing on ensuring a consistent architecture, the effective functioning of individual components and continually investigating and leveraging new technologies being developed
- IT Service Management – focusing on executing and performing the processes that optimize the cost and quality of service delivered
- Organization – focusing on the capabilities being provided that enable the business to meet its objectives, enhanced productivity for users and support for future business growth.

7.3 Event Management

The goal of Event Management is to provide the capability to detect events, make sense of them and determine the appropriate control action. Event Management is therefore the basis for Operational Monitoring and Control.

Event Management should be utilized to detect and communicate operational information as well as warnings and exceptions, so that input can be provided for reporting the service achievements and quality levels provided. It may be used for automating routine activities such as backups and batch processing, or dynamic roles for balancing demand for services across multiple infrastructure items/sources to improve performance.

- Event Management can be applied to any aspect of Service Management that needs to be controlled and which can be automated. These include:
- CIs - to provide visibility of functioning and failing components, or to understand when other changes have occurred in the infrastructure
- Environmental conditions – such as increases in the temperature of servers and facilities
- Software license monitoring – used to maintain optimum licensing utilization
- Security – to perform security checks and to detect exceptions or intrusions
- Normal activity – such as tracking the activity and performance of an IT service.

It is important to note the difference between monitoring and Event Management. While the two areas are related, Event Management focuses on the generation and detection of notifications about the status of the IT infrastructure and services. Monitoring on the other hand has a broader scope, which will include monitoring CIs that do not generate events or alerts. So when implementing Event Management, consideration should be made as to what monitoring activities and techniques should be interfaced to generate alerts and notifications that will provide value to the IT groups and wider organization.

Level 1 – Performed (Ad-hoc)	Y	N
There is some level of event monitoring and alert generation occurring across the organization.		M
Mechanisms are in place to detect service affecting events, so that an incident can be logged and appropriate correction action taken.		M
There are some thresholds in place to identify potential disruptions (e.g. caused by slow performance, 10% remaining capacity on storage device etc.) and warn the appropriate group/individual.		
Measures have been taken to filter events so that neither too many or too little alerts are being generated.		
Events that show normal operation (information events) are captured where necessary.		
Minimum score to achieve this level: **'Y' for all mandatory ('M') questions** **+ 1 other 'Y' answer**		

Level 2 – Managed	Y	N
There is a formal policy and guidelines defined for Event Management to be used in the organization.		M
Critical systems and devices are monitored to detect events occurring.		M
Training or awareness sessions have been conducted or made available electronically for staff, providing guidelines and instructions for how to employ the Event Management process.		M
The definition of an Event is clearly understood and distinguished from an incident, problem or service request.		M
There are guidelines defined for a number of roles and responsibilities associated with Event Management.		M
Information and guidelines for event monitoring, thresholds and corrective actions are provided by the service/system designers and architects.		
There are systems that provide capabilities for logging and storing events, and generating alerts.		
There are documented guidelines for when and how an incident should be logged as a result of exception events.		
Event data is used by design processes (e.g. Capacity and Availability Management) when formulating the design of a service or service change.		
Minimum score to achieve this level: **'Y' for all mandatory ('M') questions** **+ 2 other 'Y'** **answers**		

Level 3 – Defined	Y	N
Each infrastructure or application team have documented the Event Management systems being used by their team.		M
SLAs are used to design safeguards for services, ensuring that wherever possible, warnings are generated to notify of a potential breach.		M
A number of auto-response workflows have been implemented, allowing automated actions and checks to be performed without human intervention.		M
A range of communication systems are used for the transmission of alerts, including: email, SMS and the built-in messaging features of the ITSM tool(s).		M
Clear roles and responsibilities have been identified, defined, documented and appointed for the Event Management process.		M
The Configuration Management System is used to relate current and historical events with Configuration Items.		
Ownership is assigned and maintained for any escalated events.		
An operational team completes a regular health check of the IT infrastructure at least weekly, checking event records as part of the assessment.		
Event Management provides data to Release & Deployment during the distribution and early life of a release.		
The Information Security Management policy defines what security and access events must be recorded, and what follow-up actions are required.		
Event Management provides data to Capacity Management and Availability Management for both design and operational activities.		

Where the response to an event requires a standard change, there is a document procedure describing the steps to be taken.		
Minimum score to achieve this level: **'Y' for all mandatory ('M') questions** **+ 3 other 'Y'** **answers**		

Level 4 – Quantitatively Managed	Y	N
Relative standards and other quality criteria applicable for the registration of events and any follow-up actions are made clear to the Event Management team.		M
The organization will set and review targets or objectives for Event Management on a regular basis.		M
Regular reviews are held to determine shortfalls or weak areas of Event Management, using Incident and Problem data to guide improvement actions.		M
Incidents are tracked to ensure that resolution timeframes documented in SLAs are met, with any potential breaches being flagged and escalated to the appropriate party for resolution.		
Reports are regularly produced that shows how Event Management is contributing to the reduction in number and impact of service disruptions.		
The process owner will sample random event records to determine process compliance.		

Copyright The Art of Service │ Brisbane, Australia │ Email: service@theartofservice.com
Web: http://theartofservice.com │ eLearning: http://theartofservice.org │ Phone: +61 (0)7 3252 2055

Trends in the workload of Event Management is reported on and utilized to identify the staffing requirements for various work periods.		
Actions are taken to identify and reduce the number of 'false alerts' being generated.		
Minimum score to achieve this level: **'Y' for all mandatory ('M') questions** **+ 2 other 'Y'** **answers**	

Level 5 – Optimizing	Y	N
The cost and value of Event Management is quantified: this is used to assist in calculating and validating the Total Cost of Ownership (TCO) of services.		M
There is a mechanism for staff to document areas of weakness for Event Management, such as devices or components without event detection capabilities. Regular reviews seek to take corrective action if justified.		M
Event Management provides data related to Service Validation & Testing in order to better support future test designs and test models.		
Event Management provides data for process and service improvement initiatives.		
Incident Management provides Incident reference information to Event Management for Event/Incident cross reference. This seeks to enhance the early detection and resolution of exceptions.		

Minimum score to achieve this level: ('M') questions answer	'Y' for all mandatory + 1 other 'Y'	

7.4 Incident Management

The goal of Incident Management is to restore normal service operation as quickly as possible and minimize the adverse impact on business operations, thus ensuring that the best possible levels of service quality and availability are maintained. Normal service operation is defined as operating within the agreed Service Level Agreement (SLA) limits.

Incident Management can be utilized to manage any event which disrupts, or has the potential to disrupt an IT service and associated business processes. Careful distinction needs to be made between the role of Event Management and Incident Management, as only events that indicate exception to normal service operation and are determined by the Event Correlation engine to be significant are escalated to Incident Management. This means that incident records may be generated as a result of:

- End users calling the Service Desk to notify of a disruption to their normal use of IT services
- Events representing an exception that are resolved using automated means, with an associated incident record also being generated for informational purposes
- An IT staff member noticing that a component of the IT infrastructure is behaving abnormally, despite no current impact on the end user community
- An end user logging an incident using self help means, which is then resolved by IT operations staff
- An external supplier observes that a portion of the IT infrastructure under their control is experiencing issues, and logs a incident ticket via email.

While the process of Request Fulfillment does typically operate in a similar fashion to Incident Management, a service request does not involve any (potential) disruption to an IT service.

Level 1 – Performed (Ad-hoc)	Y	N
Incident records are logged and maintained for all reported incidents.		M
Incident Management exists as a consistent and repeatable process across our organization.		M
There is a defined method for calculating incident priority that is based on the relative business impact and urgency of the disruption.		
Incident Management provides the Service Desk or Customer/User with progress updates on the status of incidents (or the user can view the incident record via self-help).		
Incident Management uses consistent methods to confirm closure of the incident.		
Minimum score to achieve this level: **'Y' for all mandatory ('M') questions** **+ 1 other 'Y' answer**		

Level 2 – Managed	Y	N
There is a procedure or system for classifying incidents, with a detailed set of categorization and prioritization codes.		M
An incident database or ticketing system is maintained to record details for all reported incidents.		M
Training or awareness sessions have been conducted or made available electronically for staff, providing guidelines and instructions for how to employ the Incident Management process.		M

The definition of a Major Incident based on impact and urgency is clearly understood. A procedure for handling a Major Incident is defined, documented and followed.		M
There are guidelines defined for a number of roles and responsibilities associated with Incident Management.		M
Response and resolution times for incidents are defined in accordance with agreed targets documented in Service Level Agreements (SLAs).		
Incident managers are empowered to enforce agreed customer service levels with second line support and third party suppliers.		
An Incident Management process owner with accountability for the process across the organization has been appointed.		
A policy exists that documents rules for escalation to second-line and third-line resolver groups.		
Minimum score to achieve this level: **'Y' for all mandatory ('M') questions** **+ 2 other 'Y'** **answers**		

Level 3 – Defined	Y	N
The definition of an Incident is clearly understood as distinct and separate from a Problem; this definition is applied consistently across the organization.		M
All Incidents are assigned a priority according to a clearly defined and understood prioritization coding system based on impact and urgency.		M
New Incidents are matched with previously detected incidents, problems or known errors.		M
A number of Incident models have been defined and documented to provide a consistent approach for frequently recurring Incidents.		M
Clear roles and responsibilities have been identified, defined, documented and appointed for the Incident Management process.		M
All staff involved in incident management have access to relevant information such as known errors, problem resolutions and the configuration management system (CMS).		M
Each support group has and follows clearly defined and documented procedures to manage incidents escalated to that group.		
Ownership of an incident initiated from a user remains with the Service Desk, even when it has been escalated to a higher-level support group.		
Where an immediate resolution is not known for unmatched incidents, clearly defined activities for investigation and diagnosis activities exist.		
Prior to Incident closure, categorization codes are updated if the incident was initially categorized incorrectly.		

There is a documented policy governing whether an incident can be reopened after its initial closure.		
There is a consolidated system used to manage all incident records and the associated references to problems, known errors and change records.		
Where an incident resolution requires a normal change, a Request for Change (RFC) is raised and subsequently handled by Change Management.		
Minimum score to achieve this level: **'Y' for all mandatory ('M') questions** **+ 3 other 'Y'** **answers**		

Level 4 – Quantitatively Managed	Y	N
Relative standards and other quality criteria applicable for the registration of incidents and for call handling are made clear to the incident management team.		M
The organization will set and review targets or objectives for incident management on a regular basis.		M
Surveys are conducted to measure the user/customer satisfaction with the handling of incidents by the IT service provider.		M
Incidents are tracked to ensure that resolution timeframes documented in SLAs are met, with any potential breaches being flagged and escalated to the appropriate party for resolution.		
Reports are regularly produced that shows the percentage of incidents resolved at the first-line or second-line support groups.		

The Incident Manager will review sample incident records to review compliance to the defined process/procedures and quality standards.		
Trends in the workload of incident management is reported on and utilized to identify the staffing requirements for various work periods.		
Actions are taken to identify and reduce the number of incidents from users that bypass the Service Desk or self-help system.		
Minimum score to achieve this level: **'Y' for all mandatory ('M') questions** **+ 2 other 'Y'** **answers**		

Level 5 – Optimizing	Y	N
The costs of incidents are tracked; this information is included in assessing the Total Cost of Ownership of Services.		M
Reviews seek to identify recurring incidents that could be resolved by the user themselves using self-help mechanisms.		M
Incident Management provides evidence of incidents related to releases in order to better support future test designs and test models.		
Incident Management provides data for process and service improvement initiatives.		
Incident Management provides Incident reference information to Event Management for Event/Incident cross reference. This seeks to enhance the early detection and resolution of exceptions.		

Minimum score to achieve this level: 'Y' for all mandatory ('M') questions + 1 other 'Y' answer	

7.5 *Problem Management*

Problem Management is responsible for managing lifecycle of all problems. The primary objectives of Problem Management are:

- To prevent problems and resulting incidents from happening
- To eliminate recurring incidents
- To minimize the impact of incidents that cannot be prevented.

Clear distinction should be made between the purpose, scope and activities of Problem Management and those of Incident Management. In many cases staff may not clearly understand the distinction, and as a result not utilize their efforts in the most effective and efficient manner.

For most implementations of Problem Management the scope includes:

- The activities required to diagnose the root cause of incidents and to determine the resolution to those problems
- Activities that ensure that the resolution is implemented through the appropriate control procedures, usually through interfaces with Change Management and Release & Deployment Management
- Proactive activities that eliminate errors in the infrastructure before they result in incidents and impact on the business and end users.

Level 1 – Performed (Ad-hoc)	Y	N
Problem records are logged and maintained for all identified problems.		M
Problem Management exists as a consistent and repeatable process across our organization.		M
There is a defined method for calculating incident priority that is based on the relative impact, costs to identify and fix the problem and whether there is an existing workaround.		
Problem Management proactively manages Known Errors to aid Incident Management in the efficient resolution of related incident.		
Problem Management submits an RFC to Change Management to remove a Known Error in the production environment.		
Minimum score to achieve this level: **'Y' for all mandatory ('M') questions** **+ 1 other 'Y' answer**		

Level 2 – Managed	Y	N
There is a procedure or system for classifying problems, with a detailed set of categorization and prioritization codes.		M
A database or ticketing system is maintained to record details for all identified problems and Known Errors.		M

Training or awareness sessions have been conducted or made available electronically for staff, providing guidelines and instructions for how to employ the Problem Management process.		**M**
There are clear guidelines instructing staff about when and how a problem record should be created.		**M**
Clear roles and responsibilities have been identified, defined, documented and appointed for the Problem Management process.		**M**
There are guidelines that are defined to assist in the investigation and diagnosis of problems.		
Time and resources are made available to focus on either Reactive or Proactive Problem Management.		
A Problem Management process owner with accountability for the process across the organization has been appointed.		
A policy exists that documents rules for accepting and managing Known Errors related to a release.		
Minimum score to achieve this level: **'Y' for all mandatory ('M') questions** **+ 2 other 'Y'** **answers**		

Level 3 – Defined	Y	N
A policy exists that documents when and how a problem record should be created and which roles can perform this action.		M
Procedures define the steps to be taken for recording, classification, updating, escalation, resolution and closure of all problems		M
Problem Management has a defined guidelines and procedures for both Reactive AND Proactive Problem Management		M
There are documented guidelines to assist in evaluating whether an RFC should be raised to remove a Known Error.		M
There are one or more defined and documented methodologies used for Problem Investigation (e.g. Kepner Tregoe, Pareto Analysis, Pain-Value Analysis etc.).		M
There are effective mechanisms in place that ensure that the required stakeholders (various IT staff, teams and suppliers) are involved in Problem Management when required.		M
There is a defined set of procedures and guidelines used to review Major Problems.		
Ownership of an incident initiated from a user remains with the Service Desk, even when it has been escalated to a higher-level support group.		
Problem Management provides feedback to Availability Management and Capacity Management for assisting in capacity planning or initiatives to improve availability.		
Changes submitted by Problem Management document the resources required, risk and overall justification for the respective Change.		

	Y	N
Problem Management uses information from the Configuration Management System (CMS) to assist in the investigation and resolution of problems.		
SLAs are used to assist in the prioritization of problem records.		
Time and resources are made available for the employment of both Reactive AND Proactive Problem Management.		
There are defined guidelines used for the approval of workarounds before they are accepted into the Known Error Database or integrated ITSM tool.		
There is a Problem category for managing any security issues.		
Minimum score to achieve this level: **'Y' for all mandatory ('M') questions** **+ 4 other 'Y' answers**		

Level 4 – Quantitatively Managed	Y	N
Relative standards and other quality criteria applicable for the registration of problem records and for the associated investigation are made clear to the problem management team.		M
The organization will set and review targets or objectives for Problem Management on a regular basis.		M
Regular metrics are produced showing how Problem Management is contributing to the prevention and efficient resolution of incidents.		M
Problem and Known Error records are tracked to maintain an understanding of their progression and priority.		

Reports are regularly produced that shows the contribution of Proactive Problem Management, such as an overall decline in the number of incidents being reported.		
The costs for Problem Management analysis and resolution activities are understood.		
The Problem Manager will review sample problem and Known Error records to review compliance to the defined process/procedures and quality standards.		
Trends in the workload of Problem Management is reported on and utilized to identify the staffing requirements for both Reactive AND Proactive Problem Management.		
Minimum score to achieve this level: **'Y' for all mandatory ('M') questions** **+ 2 other 'Y'** **answer**		

Level 5 – Optimizing	Y	N
The costs of problems and Known Errors are tracked; this information is included in assessing the Total Cost of Ownership of Services.		M
Reviews seek to improve the investigation and diagnosis methods used in determining the root-cause of the problem.		M
Collaboration between Incident Management, Problem Management and Release & Deployment Management is facilitated to optimize improvements being made across the processes.		
Problem Management provides data for process and service improvement initiatives.		

Event, Incident and Problem data is used for Proactive Problem Management.		
Performance and demand of services and systems are enhanced using Problem Management data.		
Minimum score to achieve this level: **'Y' for all mandatory ('M') questions** **+ 2 other 'Y'** **answer**	

7.6 Request Fulfillment

Request Fulfillment is concerned with fulfilling requests from the end user community using consistent and repeatable methods. The objectives include:

- To provide a channel for users to request and receive standard services for which a pre-defined approval (from Change Management) qualification exists
- To provide information to users and customers about the availability of services and the procedure for obtaining them
- To source and deliver the components of requested standard services
- To assist with general information, complaints or comments.

The scope of Request Fulfillment is influenced heavily by the success of Change Management and what types of pre-approved changes can be effectively managed, controlled and implemented by the IT department. As part of continual improvement, the scope of Request Fulfillment should grow over time as maturity develops for Service Requests, including:

- Users and customers asking questions, providing comments and making complaints
- Users seeking changes to their access levels (utilizes Access Management)
- Users wishing to have common services and applications installed for their use.

Many elements of Request Fulfillment may be automated through the use of self-help such as websites and user applications, with manual activities being used where necessary to fulfill the request.

Standard Change: A pre-approved Change that is low risk, relatively common and follows a procedure or work instruction. There may still be authorization from other groups such as Human Resources; however Change Management will not need to approve each execution of the standard change.

Level 1 – Performed (Ad-hoc)	Y	N
There is a repeatable and consistent process used for managing Service Requests from the end user community.		M
There is a mechanism for recording and tracking Service Requests throughout their lifecycle.		M
There is an agreed method for calculating the priority of the Service Request based on the relative business need, urgency and resources required for fulfillment.		
There is at least some approval mechanism used to verify whether a Service Request should be fulfilled (e.g. financial, line management etc.)		
The Request Fulfillment process is used to manage all user requests not relating to a service disruption (i.e. incident), including questions, complaints, hardware and application requests, and requests for modification of access.		
Minimum score to achieve this level: 'Y' for all mandatory ('M') questions **+ 1 other 'Y' answer**		

Level 2 – Managed	Y	N
There is a procedure or system for menu selection, allowing a user or Service Desk analyst to provide input for the request to be routed to the appropriate fulfillment team.		M
There is a set of documented procedures documenting how different Service Requests should be approved, escalated and fulfilled.		M
Training or awareness sessions have been conducted or made available electronically for staff, providing guidelines and instructions for how to employ the Request Fulfillment process.		M
There is a defined procedure for closing Service Requests.		M
Clear roles and responsibilities have been identified, defined, documented and appointed for the Request Fulfillment process.		M
SLAs are used to determine appropriate response and fulfillment timeframes.		
Time and resources are made available for the appropriate engagement of Request Fulfillment.		
A process owner with accountability for the process across the organization has been appointed.		
Details of the various Service Requests that can be submitted are made available to customers and users.		
Minimum score to achieve this level: **'Y' for all mandatory ('M') questions** **+ 2 other 'Y'** **answers**		

Level 3 – Defined	Y	N
Documentation exists that states the goals, objectives and activities and procedures of the Request Fulfillment process.		M
The Service Catalogue is used to define the outcomes for customers and users from which Service Requests are derived.		M
There are a range of pre-defined Service Request models, that document the different steps to take for different types of requests (e.g. provisioning a desktop or provisioning standard applications).		M
There are documented guidelines to assist in evaluating whether an RFC should be raised to in relation to the Service Request.		M
There is a method for associating the relevant cost-centre for chargeback or accounting purposes.		M
The Service Desk acts as the primary point of contact for all Service Requests, escalating them to other fulfillment teams when required.		M
There is a procedure for raising a Service Request when necessary for resolution of an incident.		
There is a survey mechanism that allows the user/customer to provide feedback (satisfaction level) about the Request Fulfillment process.		
Release & Deployment makes pre-approved Release Packages available to be provisioned by Request Fulfillment.		
The Configuration Management System is updated accordingly throughout the fulfillment of a Service Request.		
When a Service Request relates to the provision of applications, checks are made to ensure there is sufficient availability of software licenses.		

Copyright The Art of Service | Brisbane, Australia | Email:service@theartofservice.com
Web: http://theartofservice.com | eLearning: http://theartofservice.org | Phone: +61 (0)7 3252 2055

Change Management regularly provides new and updated Standard Changes to be handled as a Service Request.		
There is a range of self-help available to users (e.g. via the internet or intranet) that enables the user to log and/or view Service Requests.		
There are a number of pre-defined workflows built into the ITSM tool used to manage Service Requests, automating parts or all of the fulfillment process.		
Service Level Agreements clearly define the expected fulfillment timeframes for different Service Requests.		
Request Fulfillment is appropriately integrated with Access Management to ensure the Information Security Policy is enforced.		
Minimum score to achieve this level: **'Y' for all mandatory ('M') questions** **+ 5 other 'Y'** **answers**		

Level 4 – Quantitatively Managed	Y	N
Relative standards and other quality criteria applicable for the registration of Service Requests and any follow-up actions is documented and made available for all teams.		M
The organization will set and review performance targets or objectives for Request Fulfillment on a regular basis.		M
Regular surveys are conducted to measure the customer and user satisfaction of the Request Fulfillment Process.		M
Regular reports are used to understand the volume of different types of Service Requests.		
Reports are regularly produced that shows the utilization of self-help for Request Fulfillment.		
The cost of provisioning each type of Service Request is understood.		
The Request Fulfillment Manager will review sample Service Request records to review compliance to the defined process/procedures and quality standards.		
Trends in the workload of Request Fulfillment is reported on and utilized to identify the future staffing requirements.		
Minimum score to achieve this level: 'Y' for all mandatory ('M') questions ** + 2 other 'Y' answer**		

Copyright The Art of Service │ Brisbane, Australia │ Email:service@theartofservice.com
Web: http://theartofservice.com │ eLearning: http://theartofservice.org │ Phone: +61 (0)7 3252 2055

Level 5 – Optimizing	Y	N
The costs of managing Service Requests are tracked; this information is included in assessing the Total Cost of Ownership of Services.		M
Reviews seek to improve the most frequently occurring Service Requests by making self-help available to users and building automation into the process workflow.		M
Feedback from Service Level Management is used to improve the Request Fulfillment process from the customer perspective.		
Request Fulfillment provides data for process and service improvement initiatives.		
Reviews are held with Change Management to review the list of standard changes; adding, changing or removing items as appropriate.		
Request Fulfillment provides input into the development of a service solution, so that the capabilities to make requests associated with the service are built-in.		
Minimum score to achieve this level: **'Y' for all mandatory ('M') questions** **+ 2 other 'Y' answer**		

7.7 Access Management

Access Management's primary objective is to provide capabilities for the granting of authorized users the right to use a service while preventing access to non-authorized users. In doing so, it helps to protect the confidentiality, integrity and availability (CIA) of the organization's services, assets, facilities and information.

Access Management is the operational execution of the policies, rules, processes and architectures implemented by Information Security and Availability Management within the Service Design phase. Although in many cases it is a process that is typically coordinated by the Service Desk, it can involve many different internal and external groups responsible for Service Operations.

Access Management ensures that users are given the right to use a service, but it does not ensure that this access is available at all agreed times – this is provided by Availability Management. As described above, the process is often centrally coordinated by the Service Desk (being the single point of contact with the end user community), but can involve the Technical and Application Management functions. Where access is controlled by external suppliers, interfaces need to be developed to coordinate requests for/modifications to access levels.

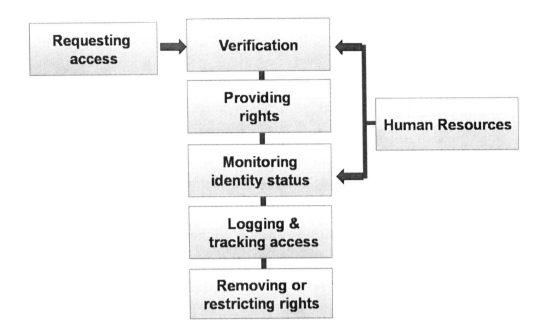

Typical Activities of Access Management

Level 1 – Performed (Ad-hoc)	Y	N
There is a repeatable and consistent process used for managing user access to services, systems and data throughout the organization.		M
There is a mechanism for recording and tracking user access events.		M
There is an agreed method for calculating the priority of the Service Request based on the relative business need, urgency and resources required for fulfillment.		
There are agreed approval mechanisms used to verify whether access should be provisioned to the user (e.g. verify with Human Resources, Line Manager, Security Team etc.)		
Access Management uses the Information Security Policy to reduce any confusion regarding the process.		
Minimum score to achieve this level: **'Y' for all mandatory ('M') questions** **+ 1 other 'Y' answer**		

Level 2 – Managed	Y	N
There is an approved information security policy that is communicated to all relevant IT personnel, customers and users.	Y	M
Requests are generated by normal Human Resources (HR) processes. This occurs when staff are hired, promoted, moved, transferred or when they leave the organization.		M

Training or awareness sessions have been conducted or made available electronically for staff, providing guidelines and instructions for how to employ the Access Management process.		M
There are supporting tools that enable staff to monitor the users' identity status, provide or restrict rights and log user access events.		M
Clear roles and responsibilities have been identified, defined, documented and appointed for the Access Management process.		M
SLAs are used to determine appropriate timeframes and communication to be conducted when managing user access requests.		
Time and resources are made available for the appropriate execution of Access Management.		
Mechanisms exist to ensure all staff hires, moves or retirements trigger the execution of Access Management.		
All exceptions or deviations from the Information Security Policy are logged and notified to the appropriate team/individuals.		
All security breaches or identified weaknesses are logged, with follow-up action taken by the appropriate team/individuals.		
Minimum score to achieve this level: **'Y' for all mandatory ('M') questions** **+ 2 other 'Y' answers**		

Level 3 – Defined	Y	N
Documentation exists that states the goals, objectives, activities and procedures of the Access Management process.		M
The impact of changes on security controls are assessed before changes are implemented.		M
Arrangements that involve external organizations having access to information systems and services based on a formal agreement that defines all necessary security requirements.		M
All security controls used in the production environment are documented.		M
There is a method for associating the relevant cost-centre for managing access requests (if required by Financial Management).		M
The Service Desk contributes to Access Management by providing an accessible channel to make access requests and by communicating any changes of the Information Security Policies to the user community.		M
There is a procedure/system defined to check for and resolve role conflicts when provisioning access.		
All security incidents are reported and recorded in line with the incident management procedure as soon as possible.		
The Configuration Management System is updated accordingly if rights and access is changed.		
When an access request relates to the provision of applications, checks are made to ensure there is sufficient availability of software licenses.		

Audits are performed on a regular basis to identify exceptions, comparing the actual rights provisioned to the documented rights and privileges (e.g. provided by HR).		
A procedure exists for handling situations where a user is under investigation (e.g. for breach of policy) but still requires some access.		
Department managers, HR staff and other relevant stakeholders have been provided education or training on how to engage with the Access Management process.		
Service Level Agreements clearly define the expected fulfillment timeframes for different access requests/activities.		
Request Fulfillment is appropriately integrated with Access Management to ensure the Information Security Policy is enforced.		
Minimum score to achieve this level: 'Y' for all mandatory ('M') questions **+ 4 other 'Y' answers**		

Level 4 – Quantitatively Managed	Y	N
Relative standards and other quality criteria applicable for the notes and documentation created within the Access Management process.		M
The organization will set and review targets or objectives for Access Management on a regular basis.		M
Regular metrics are produced showing how Access Management is ensuring compliance to the Information Security Management policy.		M
Mechanisms are in place to enable the types, volumes and impacts of security incidents and malfunctions to be quantified and monitored.		
Regular reports are produced to communicate the number and types of exceptions found when auditing access rights.		
The percentage of requests grouped by method of submission (e.g. using self-help, via the Service Desk, direct requests from management etc.) are monitored and reported.		
The operational costs associated with Access Management have been quantified.		
Measurements of user and customer satisfaction with the Access Management process are taken and reviewed.		
Performance measures such as the time taken to provide, restrict and remove rights are reviewed and reported.		
Minimum score to achieve this level: 'Y' for all mandatory ('M') questions **+ 3 other 'Y'** **answer**		

Level 5 – Optimizing	Y	N
The costs of managing access and rights for services are tracked; this information is included in assessing the Total Cost of Ownership of Services.		M
Reviews seek to improve the most frequently occurring Service Requests by making self-help available to users and building automation into the process workflow.		M
Access Management provides input to Availability Management in the design of security systems, controls and infrastructure.		M
Feedback from Service Level Management is used to improve the Access Management process from the customer perspective.		
Access Management provides data for process and service improvement initiatives.		
Reviews are held with Information Security Management to embed short-term and long-term improvements to the Information Security Policy.		
Request Fulfillment provides input into the development of a service solution, so that the capabilities to make requests associated with the service are built-in.		
Minimum score to achieve this level: **'Y' for all mandatory ('M') questions** **+ 2 other 'Y'** **answer**		

Copyright The Art of Service │ Brisbane, Australia│ Email:service@theartofservice.com
Web: http://theartofservice.com │ eLearning: http://theartofservice.org │ Phone: +61 (0)7 3252 2055

8 Further Reading

For more information on other products available from The Art of Service, you can visit our website: http://www.theartofservice.com

If you found this guide helpful, you can find more publications from The Art of Service at: http://www.amazon.com

9 Glossary

Term	Definition
Access Management	(Service Operation) The Process responsible for allowing Users to make use of IT Services, data, or other Assets. Access Management helps to protect the Confidentiality, Integrity and Availability of Assets by ensuring that only authorized Users are able to access or modify the Assets. Access Management is sometimes referred to as Rights Management or Identity Management.
Account Manager	(Service Strategy) A Role that is very similar to Business Relationship Manager, but includes more commercial aspects. Most commonly used when dealing with External Customers.
Accounting	(Service Strategy) The Process responsible for identifying actual Costs of delivering IT Services, comparing these with budgeted costs, and managing variance from the Budget.
Application Management	(Service Design) (Service Operation) The Function responsible for managing Applications throughout their Lifecycle.
Application Portfolio	(Service Design) A database or structured Document used to manage Applications throughout their Lifecycle. The Application Portfolio contains key Attributes of all Applications. The Application Portfolio is sometimes implemented as part of the Service Portfolio, or as part of the Configuration Management System.

Copyright The Art of Service │ Brisbane, Australia │ Email:service@theartofservice.com
Web: http://theartofservice.com │ eLearning: http://theartofservice.org │ Phone: +61 (0)7 3252 2055

Term	Definition
Asset	(Service Strategy) Any Resource or Capability. Assets of a Service Provider include anything that could contribute to the delivery of a Service. Assets can be one of the following types: Management, Organisation, Process, Knowledge, People, Information, Applications, Infrastructure, and Financial Capital.
Asset Management	(Service Transition) Asset Management is the Process responsible for tracking and reporting the value and ownership of financial Assets throughout their Lifecycle. Asset Management is part of an overall Service Asset and Configuration Management Process. See Asset Register.
Audit	Formal inspection and verification to check whether a Standard or set of Guidelines is being followed, that Records are accurate, or that Efficiency and Effectiveness targets are being met. An Audit may be carried out by internal or external groups. See Certification, Assessment.
Availability	(Service Design) Ability of a Configuration Item or IT Service to perform its agreed Function when required. Availability is determined by Reliability, Maintainability, Serviceability, Performance, and Security. Availability is usually calculated as a percentage. This calculation is often based on Agreed Service Time and Downtime. It is Best Practice to calculate Availability using measurements of the Business output of the IT Service.

Term	Definition
Availability Management	(Service Design) The Process responsible for defining, analysing, Planning, measuring and improving all aspects of the Availability of IT Services. Availability Management is responsible for ensuring that all IT Infrastructure, Processes, Tools, Roles etc are appropriate for the agreed Service Level Targets for Availability.
Baseline	(Continual Service Improvement) A Benchmark used as a reference point. For example: An ITSM Baseline can be used as a starting point to measure the effect of a Service Improvement Plan A Performance Baseline can be used to measure changes in Performance over the lifetime of an IT Service A Configuration Management Baseline can be used to enable the IT Infrastructure to be restored to a known Configuration if a Change or Release fails
Business Capacity Management (BCM)	(Service Design) In the context of ITSM, Business Capacity Management is the Activity responsible for understanding future Business Requirements for use in the Capacity Plan. See Service Capacity Management.
Business Case	(Service Strategy) Justification for a significant item of expenditure. Includes information about Costs, benefits, options, issues, Risks, and possible problems. See Cost Benefit Analysis.

Term	Definition
Business Continuity Management (BCM)	(Service Design) The Business Process responsible for managing Risks that could seriously impact the Business. BCM safeguards the interests of key stakeholders, reputation, brand and value creating activities. The BCM Process involves reducing Risks to an acceptable level and planning for the recovery of Business Processes should a disruption to the Business occur. BCM sets the Objectives, Scope and Requirements for IT Service Continuity Management.
Business Continuity Plan (BCP)	(Service Design) A Plan defining the steps required to Restore Business Processes following a disruption. The Plan will also identify the triggers for Invocation, people to be involved, communications etc. IT Service Continuity Plans form a significant part of Business Continuity Plans.
Business Impact Analysis (BIA)	(Service Strategy) BIA is the Activity in Business Continuity Management that identifies Vital Business Functions and their dependencies. These dependencies may include Suppliers, people, other Business Processes, IT Services etc. BIA defines the recovery requirements for IT Services. These requirements include Recovery Time Objectives, Recovery Point Objectives and minimum Service Level Targets for each IT Service.
Business Relationship Manager (BRM)	(Service Strategy) A Role responsible for maintaining the Relationship with one or more Customers. This Role is often combined with the Service Level Manager Role. See Account Manager.

Term	Definition
Call Centre	(Service Operation) An Organisation or Business Unit which handles large numbers of incoming and outgoing telephone calls. See Service Desk.
Capability	(Service Strategy) The ability of an Organisation, person, Process, Application, Configuration Item or IT Service to carry out an Activity. Capabilities are intangible Assets of an Organisation. See Resource.
Capacity	(Service Design) The maximum Throughput that a Configuration Item or IT Service can deliver whilst meeting agreed Service Level Targets. For some types of CI, Capacity may be the size or volume, for example a disk drive.
Capacity Management	(Service Design) The Process responsible for ensuring that the Capacity of IT Services and the IT Infrastructure is able to deliver agreed Service Level Targets in a Cost Effective and timely manner. Capacity Management considers all Resources required to deliver the IT Service, and plans for short, medium and long term Business Requirements.
Change	(Service Transition) The addition, modification or removal of anything that could have an effect on IT Services. The Scope should include all IT Services, Configuration Items, Processes, Documentation etc.

Term	Definition
Change Advisory Board (CAB)	(Service Transition) A group of people that advises the Change Manager in the Assessment, prioritisation and scheduling of Changes. This board is usually made up of representatives from all areas within the IT Service Provider, the Business, and Third Parties such as Suppliers.
Change Management	(Service Transition) The Process responsible for controlling the Lifecycle of all Changes. The primary objective of Change Management is to enable beneficial Changes to be made, with minimum disruption to IT Services.
Change Model	(Service Transition) A repeatable way of dealing with a particular Category of Change. A Change Model defines specific pre-defined steps that will be followed for a Change of this Category. Change Models may be very simple, with no requirement for approval (e.g. Password Reset) or may be very complex with many steps that require approval (e.g. major software Release). See Standard Change, Change Advisory Board.
Cold Standby	Synonym for Gradual Recovery.
Configuration Baseline	(Service Transition) A Baseline of a Configuration that has been formally agreed and is managed through the Change Management process. A Configuration Baseline is used as a basis for future Builds, Releases and Changes.

Term	Definition
Configuration Item (CI)	(Service Transition) Any Component that needs to be managed in order to deliver an IT Service. Information about each CI is recorded in a Configuration Record within the Configuration Management System and is maintained throughout its Lifecycle by Configuration Management. CIs are under the control of Change Management. CIs typically include IT Services, hardware, software, buildings, people, and formal documentation such as Process documentation and SLAs.
Configuration Management	(Service Transition) The Process responsible for maintaining information about Configuration Items required to deliver an IT Service, including their Relationships. This information is managed throughout the Lifecycle of the CI. Configuration Management is part of an overall Service Asset and Configuration Management Process.
Configuration Management Database (CMDB)	(Service Transition) A database used to store Configuration Records throughout their Lifecycle. The Configuration Management System maintains one or more CMDBs, and each CMDB stores Attributes of CIs, and Relationships with other CIs.

Term	Definition
Configuration Management System (CMS)	(Service Transition) A set of tools and databases that are used to manage an IT Service Provider's Configuration data. The CMS also includes information about Incidents, Problems, Known Errors, Changes and Releases; and may contain data about employees, Suppliers, locations, Business Units, Customers and Users. The CMS includes tools for collecting, storing, managing, updating, and presenting data about all Configuration Items and their Relationships. The CMS is maintained by Configuration Management and is used by all IT Service Management Processes. See Configuration Management Database, Service Knowledge Management System.
Continual Service Improvement (CSI)	(Continual Service Improvement) A stage in the Lifecycle of an IT Service and the title of one of the Core ITIL publications. Continual Service Improvement is responsible for managing improvements to IT Service Management Processes and IT Services. The Performance of the IT Service Provider is continually measured and improvements are made to Processes, IT Services and IT Infrastructure in order to increase Efficiency, Effectiveness, and Cost Effectiveness. See Plan-Do-Check-Act.
Cost Benefit Analysis	An Activity that analyses and compares the Costs and the benefits involved in one or more alternative courses of action. See Business Case, Net Present Value, Internal Rate of Return, Return on Investment, Value on Investment.

Term	Definition
Customer	Someone who buys goods or Services. The Customer of an IT Service Provider is the person or group who defines and agrees the Service Level Targets. The term Customers is also sometimes informally used to mean Users, for example "this is a Customer focussed Organisation".
Data-to-Information-to-Knowledge-to-Wisdom (DIKW)	A way of understanding the relationships between data, information, knowledge, and wisdom. DIKW shows how each of these builds on the others.
Definitive Media Library (DML)	(Service Transition) One or more locations in which the definitive and approved versions of all software Configuration Items are securely stored. The DML may also contain associated CIs such as licenses and documentation. The DML is a single logical storage area even if there are multiple locations. All software in the DML is under the control of Change and Release Management and is recorded in the Configuration Management System. Only software from the DML is acceptable for use in a Release.
Deliverable	Something that must be provided to meet a commitment in a Service Level Agreement or a Contract. Deliverable is also used in a more informal way to mean a planned output of any Process.

Term	Definition
Demand Management	Activities that understand and influence Customer demand for Services and the provision of Capacity to meet these demands. At a Strategic level Demand Management can involve analysis of Patterns of Business Activity and User Profiles. At a Tactical level it can involve use of Differential Charging to encourage Customers to use IT Services at less busy times. See Capacity Management.
Deming Cycle	Synonym for Plan Do Check Act.
Deployment	(Service Transition) The Activity responsible for movement of new or changed hardware, software, documentation, Process, etc to the Live Environment. Deployment is part of the Release and Deployment Management Process. See Rollout.
Downtime	(Service Design) (Service Operation) The time when a Configuration Item or IT Service is not Available during its Agreed Service Time. The Availability of an IT Service is often calculated from Agreed Service Time and Downtime.
Effectiveness	(Continual Service Improvement) A measure of whether the Objectives of a Process, Service or Activity have been achieved. An Effective Process or Activity is one that achieves its agreed Objectives. See KPI.

Term	Definition
Efficiency	(Continual Service Improvement) A measure of whether the right amount of resources have been used to deliver a Process, Service or Activity. An Efficient Process achieves its Objectives with the minimum amount of time, money, people or other resources. See KPI.
Emergency Change	(Service Transition) A Change that must be introduced as soon as possible. For example to resolve a Major Incident or implement a Security patch. The Change Management Process will normally have a specific Procedure for handling Emergency Changes. See Emergency Change Advisory Board (ECAB).
Emergency Change Advisory Board (ECAB)	(Service Transition) A sub-set of the Change Advisory Board who make decisions about high impact Emergency Changes. Membership of the ECAB may be decided at the time a meeting is called, and depends on the nature of the Emergency Change.
Error	(Service Operation) A design flaw or malfunction that causes a Failure of one or more Configuration Items or IT Services. A mistake made by a person or a faulty Process that impacts a CI or IT Service is also an Error.

Term	Definition
Escalation	(Service Operation) An Activity that obtains additional Resources when these are needed to meet Service Level Targets or Customer expectations. Escalation may be needed within any IT Service Management Process, but is most commonly associated with Incident Management, Problem Management and the management of Customer complaints. There are two types of Escalation, Functional Escalation and Hierarchic Escalation.
Evaluation	(Service Transition) The Process responsible for assessing a new or Changed IT Service to ensure that Risks have been managed and to help determine whether to proceed with the Change. Evaluation is also used to mean comparing an actual Outcome with the intended Outcome, or comparing one alternative with another.
Event	(Service Operation) A change of state which has significance for the management of a Configuration Item or IT Service. The term Event is also used to mean an Alert or notification created by any IT Service, Configuration Item or Monitoring tool. Events typically require IT Operations personnel to take actions, and often lead to Incidents being logged.
Event Management	(Service Operation) The Process responsible for managing Events throughout their Lifecycle. Event Management is one of the main Activities of IT Operations.

Term	Definition
External Service Provider	(Service Strategy) An IT Service Provider which is part of a different Organisation to their Customer. An IT Service Provider may have both Internal Customers and External Customers. See Type III Service Provider.
Facilities Management	(Service Operation) The Function responsible for managing the physical Environment where the IT Infrastructure is located. Facilities Management includes all aspects of managing the physical Environment, for example power and cooling, building Access Management, and environmental Monitoring.
Failure	(Service Operation) Loss of ability to Operate to Specification, or to deliver the required output. The term Failure may be used when referring to IT Services, Processes, Activities, Configuration Items etc. A Failure often causes an Incident.
Fault Tree Analysis (FTA)	(Service Design) (Continual Service Improvement) A technique that can be used to determine the chain of Events that leads to a Problem. Fault Tree Analysis represents a chain of Events using Boolean notation in a diagram.
Financial Management	(Service Strategy) The Function and Processes responsible for managing an IT Service Provider's Budgeting, Accounting and Charging Requirements.
Fit for Purpose	An informal term used to describe a Process, Configuration Item, IT Service etc. that is capable of meeting its Objectives or Service Levels. Being Fit for Purpose requires suitable Design, implementation, Control and maintenance.

Term	Definition
Follow the Sun	(Service Operation) A methodology for using Service Desks and Support Groups around the world to provide seamless 24 * 7 Service. Calls, Incidents, Problems and Service Requests are passed between groups in different time zones.
Help Desk	(Service Operation) A point of contact for Users to log Incidents. A Help Desk is usually more technically focussed than a Service Desk and does not provide a Single Point of Contact for all interaction. The term Help Desk is often used as a synonym for Service Desk.
Hot Standby	Synonym for Fast Recovery or Immediate Recovery.
Immediate Recovery	(Service Design) A Recovery Option which is also known as Hot Standby. Provision is made to Recover the IT Service with no loss of Service. Immediate Recovery typically uses mirroring, load balancing and split site technologies.
Incident	(Service Operation) An unplanned interruption to an IT Service or a reduction in the Quality of an IT Service. Failure of a Configuration Item that has not yet impacted Service is also an Incident. For example Failure of one disk from a mirror set.
Incident Management	(Service Operation) The Process responsible for managing the Lifecycle of all Incidents. The primary Objective of Incident Management is to return the IT Service to Users as quickly as possible.

Term	Definition
Information Security Management (ISM)	(Service Design) The Process that ensures the Confidentiality, Integrity and Availability of an Organisation's Assets, information, data and IT Services. Information Security Management usually forms part of an Organisational approach to Security Management which has a wider scope than the IT Service Provider, and includes handling of paper, building access, phone calls etc., for the entire Organisation.
Information Technology (IT)	The use of technology for the storage, communication or processing of information. The technology typically includes computers, telecommunications, Applications and other software. The information may include Business data, voice, images, video, etc. Information Technology is often used to support Business Processes through IT Services.
Intermediate Recovery	(Service Design) A Recovery Option which is also known as Warm Standby. Provision is made to Recover the IT Service in a period of time between 24 and 72 hours. Intermediate Recovery typically uses a shared Portable or Fixed Facility that has computer Systems and network Components. The hardware and software will need to be configured, and data will need to be restored, as part of the IT Service Continuity Plan.
Internal Customer	A Customer who works for the same Business as the IT Service Provider. See Internal Service Provider, External Customer.

Copyright The Art of Service | Brisbane, Australia | Email:service@theartofservice.com
Web: http://theartofservice.com | eLearning: http://theartofservice.org | Phone: +61 (0)7 3252 2055

Term	Definition
Internal Service Provider	(Service Strategy) An IT Service Provider which is part of the same Organisation as their Customer. An IT Service Provider may have both Internal Customers and External Customers. See Type I Service Provider, Type II Service Provider, Insource.
Ishikawa Diagram	(Service Operation) (Continual Service Improvement) A technique that helps a team to identify all the possible causes of a Problem. Originally devised by Kaoru Ishikawa, the output of this technique is a diagram that looks like a fishbone.
ISO 9000	A generic term that refers to a number of international Standards and Guidelines for Quality Management Systems. See http://www.iso.org/ for more information. See ISO.
ISO 9001	An international Standard for Quality Management Systems. See ISO 9000, Standard.
ISO/IEC 17799	(Continual Service Improvement) ISO Code of Practice for Information Security Management. See Standard.
ISO/IEC 20000	ISO Specification and Code of Practice for IT Service Management. ISO/IEC 20000 is aligned with ITIL Best Practice.
ISO/IEC 27001	(Service Design) (Continual Service Improvement) ISO Specification for Information Security Management. The corresponding Code of Practice is ISO/IEC 17799. See Standard.

Term	Definition
IT Service Continuity Management (ITSCM)	(Service Design) The Process responsible for managing Risks that could seriously impact IT Services. ITSCM ensures that the IT Service Provider can always provide minimum agreed Service Levels, by reducing the Risk to an acceptable level and Planning for the Recovery of IT Services. ITSCM should be designed to support Business Continuity Management.
IT Service Management (ITSM)	The implementation and management of Quality IT Services that meet the needs of the Business. IT Service Management is performed by IT Service Providers through an appropriate mix of people, Process and Information Technology. See Service Management.
IT Service Management Forum (itSMF)	The IT Service Management Forum is an independent Organisation dedicated to promoting a professional approach to IT Service Management. The itSMF is a not-for-profit membership Organisation with representation in many countries around the world (itSMF Chapters). The itSMF and its membership contribute to the development of ITIL and associated IT Service Management Standards. See http://www.itsmf.com/ for more information.
ITIL	A set of Best Practice guidance for IT Service Management. ITIL is owned by the OGC and consists of a series of publications giving guidance on the provision of Quality IT Services, and on the Processes and facilities needed to support them. See http://www.itil.co.uk/ for more information.

Term	Definition
Kepner & Tregoe Analysis	(Service Operation) (Continual Service Improvement) A structured approach to Problem solving. The Problem is analysed in terms of what, where, when and extent. Possible causes are identified. The most probable cause is tested. The true cause is verified.
Key Performance Indicator (KPI)	(Continual Service Improvement) A Metric that is used to help manage a Process, IT Service or Activity. Many Metrics may be measured, but only the most important of these are defined as KPIs and used to actively manage and report on the Process, IT Service or Activity. KPIs should be selected to ensure that Efficiency, Effectiveness, and Cost Effectiveness are all managed. See Critical Success Factor.
Knowledge Management	(Service Transition) The Process responsible for gathering, analysing, storing and sharing knowledge and information within an Organisation. The primary purpose of Knowledge Management is to improve Efficiency by reducing the need to rediscover knowledge. See Data-to-Information-to-Knowledge-to-Wisdom, Service Knowledge Management System.
Known Error	(Service Operation) A Problem that has a documented Root Cause and a Workaround. Known Errors are created and managed throughout their Lifecycle by Problem Management. Known Errors may also be identified by Development or Suppliers.

Term	Definition
Known Error Database (KEDB)	(Service Operation) A database containing all Known Error Records. This database is created by Problem Management and used by Incident and Problem Management. The Known Error Database is part of the Service Knowledge Management System.
Lifecycle	The various stages in the life of an IT Service, Configuration Item, Incident, Problem, Change etc. The Lifecycle defines the Categories for Status and the Status transitions that are permitted. For example: The Lifecycle of an Application includes Requirements, Design, Build, Deploy, Operate, Optimise. The Expanded Incident Lifecycle includes Detect, Respond, Diagnose, Repair, Recover, Restore. The lifecycle of a Server may include: Ordered, Received, In Test, Live, Disposed etc.
Major Incident	(Service Operation) The highest Category of Impact for an Incident. A Major Incident results in significant disruption to the Business.
Manual Workaround	A Workaround that requires manual intervention. Manual Workaround is also used as the name of a Recovery Option in which The Business Process Operates without the use of IT Services. This is a temporary measure and is usually combined with another Recovery Option.

Term	Definition
Mean Time Between Failures (MTBF)	(Service Design) A Metric for measuring and reporting Reliability. MTBF is the average time that a Configuration Item or IT Service can perform its agreed Function without interruption. This is measured from when the CI or IT Service starts working, until it next fails.
Mean Time Between Service Incidents (MTBSI)	(Service Design) A Metric used for measuring and reporting Reliability. MTBSI is the mean time from when a System or IT Service fails, until it next fails. MTBSI is equal to MTBF + MTRS.
Mean Time To Repair (MTTR)	The average time taken to repair a Configuration Item or IT Service after a Failure. MTTR is measured from when the CI or IT Service fails until it is Repaired. MTTR does not include the time required to Recover or Restore. MTTR is sometimes incorrectly used to mean Mean Time to Restore Service.
Mean Time to Restore Service (MTRS)	The average time taken to Restore a Configuration Item or IT Service after a Failure. MTRS is measured from when the CI or IT Service fails until it is fully Restored and delivering its normal functionality. See Maintainability, Mean Time to Repair.
Modelling	A technique that is used to predict the future behaviour of a System, Process, IT Service, Configuration Item etc. Modelling is commonly used in Financial Management, Capacity Management and Availability Management.

Term	Definition
Office of Government Commerce (OGC)	OGC owns the ITIL brand (copyright and trademark). OGC is a UK Government department that supports the delivery of the government's procurement agenda through its work in collaborative procurement and in raising levels of procurement skills and capability with departments. It also provides support for complex public sector projects.
Operational Level Agreement (OLA)	(Service Design) (Continual Service Improvement) An Agreement between an IT Service Provider and another part of the same Organisation. An OLA supports the IT Service Provider's delivery of IT Services to Customers. The OLA defines the goods or Services to be provided and the responsibilities of both parties. For example there could be an OLA between the IT Service Provider and a procurement department to obtain hardware in agreed times between the Service Desk and a Support Group to provide Incident Resolution in agreed times. See Service Level Agreement.
Pareto Principle	(Service Operation) A technique used to prioritise Activities. The Pareto Principle says that 80% of the value of any Activity is created with 20% of the effort. Pareto Analysis is also used in Problem Management to prioritise possible Problem causes for investigation.

Term	Definition
Pattern of Business Activity (PBA)	(Service Strategy) A Workload profile of one or more Business Activities. Patterns of Business Activity are used to help the IT Service Provider understand and plan for different levels of Business Activity. See User Profile.
Performance Anatomy	(Service Strategy) An approach to Organisational Culture that integrates, and actively manages, leadership and strategy, people development, technology enablement, performance management and innovation.
Plan-Do-Check-Act	(Continual Service Improvement) A four stage cycle for Process management, attributed to Edward Deming. Plan-Do-Check-Act is also called the Deming Cycle. PLAN: Design or revise Processes that support the IT Services. DO: Implement the Plan and manage the Processes. CHECK: Measure the Processes and IT Services, compare with Objectives and produce reports ACT: Plan and implement Changes to improve the Processes.
PMBOK	A Project management Standard maintained and published by the Project Management Institute. PMBOK stands for Project Management Body of Knowledge. See http://www.pmi.org/ for more information. See PRINCE2.
Post Implementation Review (PIR)	A Review that takes place after a Change or a Project has been implemented. A PIR determines if the Change or Project was successful, and identifies opportunities for improvement.

Term	Definition
PRINCE2	The standard UK government methodology for Project management. See http://www.ogc.gov.uk/prince2/ for more information. See PMBOK.
Problem	(Service Operation) A cause of one or more Incidents. The cause is not usually known at the time a Problem Record is created, and the Problem Management Process is responsible for further investigation.
Problem Management	(Service Operation) The Process responsible for managing the Lifecycle of all Problems. The primary Objectives of Problem Management are to prevent Incidents from happening, and to minimise the Impact of Incidents that cannot be prevented.
Quality Assurance (QA)	(Service Transition) The Process responsible for ensuring that the Quality of a product, Service or Process will provide its intended Value.
RACI	(Service Design) (Continual Service Improvement) A Model used to help define Roles and Responsibilities. RACI stands for Responsible, Accountable, Consulted and Informed. See Stakeholder.
Recovery	(Service Design) (Service Operation) Returning a Configuration Item or an IT Service to a working state. Recovery of an IT Service often includes recovering data to a known consistent state. After Recovery, further steps may be needed before the IT Service can be made available to the Users (Restoration).

Term	Definition
Release	(Service Transition) A collection of hardware, software, documentation, Processes or other Components required to implement one or more approved Changes to IT Services. The contents of each Release are managed, Tested, and Deployed as a single entity.
Release and Deployment Management	(Service Transition) The Process responsible for both Release Management and Deployment.
Release Management	(Service Transition) The Process responsible for Planning, scheduling and controlling the movement of Releases to Test and Live Environments. The primary Objective of Release Management is to ensure that the integrity of the Live Environment is protected and that the correct Components are released. Release Management is part of the Release and Deployment Management Process.
Request for Change (RFC)	(Service Transition) A formal proposal for a Change to be made. An RFC includes details of the proposed Change, and may be recorded on paper or electronically. The term RFC is often misused to mean a Change Record, or the Change itself.
Return on Investment (ROI)	(Service Strategy) (Continual Service Improvement) A measurement of the expected benefit of an investment. In the simplest sense it is the net profit of an investment divided by the net worth of the assets invested. See Net Present Value, Value on Investment.

Term	Definition
Risk	A possible Event that could cause harm or loss, or affect the ability to achieve Objectives. A Risk is measured by the probability of a Threat, the Vulnerability of the Asset to that Threat, and the Impact it would have if it occurred.
Risk Assessment	The initial steps of Risk Management. Analysing the value of Assets to the business, identifying Threats to those Assets, and evaluating how Vulnerable each Asset is to those Threats. Risk Assessment can be quantitative (based on numerical data) or qualitative.
Risk Management	The Process responsible for identifying, assessing and controlling Risks. See Risk Assessment.
Rollout	(Service Transition) Synonym for Deployment. Most often used to refer to complex or phased Deployments or Deployments to multiple locations.
Service	A means of delivering value to Customers by facilitating Outcomes Customers want to achieve without the ownership of specific Costs and Risks.
Service Acceptance Criteria (SAC)	(Service Transition) A set of criteria used to ensure that an IT Service meets its functionality and Quality Requirements and that the IT Service Provider is ready to Operate the new IT Service when it has been Deployed. See Acceptance.

Term	Definition
Service Asset and Configuration Management (SACM)	(Service Transition) The Process responsible for both Configuration Management and Asset Management.
Service Capacity Management (SCM)	(Service Design) (Continual Service Improvement) The Activity responsible for understanding the Performance and Capacity of IT Services. The Resources used by each IT Service and the pattern of usage over time are collected, recorded, and analysed for use in the Capacity Plan. See Business Capacity Management, Component Capacity Management.
Service Catalogue	(Service Design) A database or structured Document with information about all Live IT Services, including those available for Deployment. The Service Catalogue is the only part of the Service Portfolio published to Customers, and is used to support the sale and delivery of IT Services. The Service Catalogue includes information about deliverables, prices, contact points, ordering and request Processes. See Contract Portfolio.
Service Design	(Service Design) A stage in the Lifecycle of an IT Service. Service Design includes a number of Processes and Functions and is the title of one of the Core ITIL publications. See Design.

Term	Definition
Service Desk	(Service Operation) The Single Point of Contact between the Service Provider and the Users. A typical Service Desk manages Incidents and Service Requests, and also handles communication with the Users.
Service Knowledge Management System (SKMS)	(Service Transition) A set of tools and databases that are used to manage knowledge and information. The SKMS includes the Configuration Management System, as well as other tools and databases. The SKMS stores, manages, updates, and presents all information that an IT Service Provider needs to manage the full Lifecycle of IT Services.
Service Level Agreement (SLA)	(Service Design) (Continual Service Improvement) An Agreement between an IT Service Provider and a Customer. The SLA describes the IT Service, documents Service Level Targets, and specifies the responsibilities of the IT Service Provider and the Customer. A single SLA may cover multiple IT Services or multiple Customers. See Operational Level Agreement.
Service Level Management (SLM)	(Service Design) (Continual Service Improvement) The Process responsible for negotiating Service Level Agreements, and ensuring that these are met. SLM is responsible for ensuring that all IT Service Management Processes, Operational Level Agreements, and Underpinning Contracts, are appropriate for the agreed Service Level Targets. SLM monitors and reports on Service Levels, and holds regular Customer reviews.

Copyright The Art of Service │ Brisbane, Australia │ Email:service@theartofservice.com
Web: http://theartofservice.com │ eLearning: http://theartofservice.org │ Phone: +61 (0)7 3252 2055

Term	Definition
Service Level Package (SLP)	(Service Strategy) A defined level of Utility and Warranty for a particular Service Package. Each SLP is designed to meet the needs of a particular Pattern of Business Activity. See Line of Service.
Service Level Requirement (SLR)	(Service Design) (Continual Service Improvement) A Customer Requirement for an aspect of an IT Service. SLRs are based on Business Objectives and are used to negotiate agreed Service Level Targets.
Service Owner	(Continual Service Improvement) A Role which is accountable for the delivery of a specific IT Service.
Service Portfolio	(Service Strategy) The complete set of Services that are managed by a Service Provider. The Service Portfolio is used to manage the entire Lifecycle of all Services, and includes three Categories: Service Pipeline (proposed or in Development); Service Catalogue (Live or available for Deployment); and Retired Services. See Service Portfolio Management, Contract Portfolio.
Service Portfolio Management (SPM)	(Service Strategy) The Process responsible for managing the Service Portfolio. Service Portfolio Management considers Services in terms of the Business value that they provide.
Service Transition	(Service Transition) A stage in the Lifecycle of an IT Service. Service Transition includes a number of Processes and Functions and is the title of one of the Core ITIL publications. See Transition.

Term	Definition
Service Validation and Testing	(Service Transition) The Process responsible for Validation and Testing of a new or Changed IT Service. Service Validation and Testing ensures that the IT Service matches its Design Specification and will meet the needs of the Business.
Serviceability	(Service Design) (Continual Service Improvement) The ability of a Third Party Supplier to meet the terms of their Contract. This Contract will include agreed levels of Reliability, Maintainability or Availability for a Configuration Item.
Storage Management	(Service Operation) The Process responsible for managing the storage and maintenance of data throughout its Lifecycle.
Supplier and Contract Database (SCD)	(Service Design) A database or structured Document used to manage Supplier Contracts throughout their Lifecycle. The SCD contains key Attributes of all Contracts with Suppliers, and should be part of the Service Knowledge Management System.
Supplier Management	(Service Design) The Process responsible for ensuring that all Contracts with Suppliers support the needs of the Business, and that all Suppliers meet their contractual commitments.
SWOT Analysis	(Continual Service Improvement) A technique that reviews and analyses the internal strengths and weaknesses of an Organisation and the external opportunities and threats which it faces SWOT stands for Strengths, Weaknesses, Opportunities and Threats.

Term	Definition
Threat	Anything that might exploit a Vulnerability. Any potential cause of an Incident can be considered to be a Threat. For example a fire is a Threat that could exploit the Vulnerability of flammable floor coverings. This term is commonly used in Information Security Management and IT Service Continuity Management, but also applies to other areas such as Problem and Availability Management.
Type II Service Provider	(Service Strategy) An Internal Service Provider that provides shared IT Services to more than one Business Unit.
Underpinning Contract (UC)	(Service Design) A Contract between an IT Service Provider and a Third Party. The Third Party provides goods or Services that support delivery of an IT Service to a Customer. The Underpinning Contract defines targets and responsibilities that are required to meet agreed Service Level Targets in an SLA.
User	A person who uses the IT Service on a day-to-day basis. Users are distinct from Customers, as some Customers do not use the IT Service directly.
Value on Investment (VOI)	(Continual Service Improvement) A measurement of the expected benefit of an investment. VOI considers both financial and intangible benefits. See Return on Investment.

Term	Definition
Vital Business Function (VBF)	(Service Design) A Function of a Business Process which is critical to the success of the Business. Vital Business Functions are an important consideration of Business Continuity Management, IT Service Continuity Management and Availability Management.
Workaround	(Service Operation) Reducing or eliminating the Impact of an Incident or Problem for which a full Resolution is not yet available. For example by restarting a failed Configuration Item. Workarounds for Problems are documented in Known Error Records. Workarounds for Incidents that do not have associated Problem Records are documented in the Incident Record.

10 Index

A

B

C

D

databases   86, 127, 154, 176, 182-3, 194, 201-2, 204
delivery   33, 41, 109, 138, 177, 196, 201, 203
diagnosis   10, 13-14, 18, 23, 34, 155
DIKW (Data-to-Information-to-Knowledge-to-Wisdom)   184, 193
disruption   13-14, 18, 131, 146-7, 179, 194
documentation   17, 25, 69, 77, 84, 163, 171, 173, 180, 184-5, 199

E

education   126, 128-9, 172
efficiency   26, 138, 183, 186, 193
environment   18, 40, 42, 47, 73, 78, 111
errors   7, 10, 19, 23, 34, 43, 52, 63-4, 69, 85, 88-92, 111, 153, 186
escalation   11, 28, 148, 156, 187
Event Management   4, 10, 139-44, 146, 187
events   17, 133, 139-41, 143, 146, 159, 187, 200
exceptions   139, 146, 170, 172-3
expenditure   121, 126, 178

F

failure   13, 103, 113, 186, 188-9, 195
Fault Tree Analysis (FTA)   188
faults   22, 76
feedback   24, 156, 163, 166, 174
flyers   3, 56-7, 106
functions   92, 128, 176-7, 188, 195, 201, 203, 206

G

guidelines   135, 141, 147-8, 155-6, 162, 170, 177

H

hardware   73, 88, 121, 126, 161, 182, 190, 196, 199
HR (Human Resources)   160, 169, 172

I

implementation   4, 10, 18, 29, 38-9, 41, 62, 120, 122, 125-8, 188, 192
improvements   30-2, 116, 132-3, 183, 197
Incident Management   4-6, 13, 23, 125, 144, 146-51, 153, 158, 187, 189

R

record 70, 78, 86-9, 111, 177
recover 132, 189-90, 194-5
Release Management 184, 199
Request Fulfillment 4, 146, 160, 162-6, 172, 174
requests 18, 94, 124, 150, 160-3, 166, 169, 173-4, 199
resolution 7, 18-19, 23, 25, 35, 92, 111, 143, 149-50, 153, 156, 163, 206
resources 14, 18, 28, 112, 132, 134, 155-7, 161-2, 169-70, 177, 180, 186-7, 201
responsibilities 27, 44, 116, 125, 129, 141-2, 148-9, 155, 162, 170, 196, 198, 202, 205
RFC (Request for Change) 18, 24, 26, 92, 94-5, 150, 156, 163, 199
rights 170-4
risks 31, 35, 44, 156, 178, 187, 192, 200
ROI (Return on Investment) 183, 199, 205
root cause 6, 13, 17, 90

S

scope 3, 5, 7, 18, 49-50, 54, 68-9, 84-5, 120, 123, 128, 140, 153, 179-80, 190
security 31, 44, 73, 79, 139, 142, 170, 177
self-help 147, 160, 164-6, 173-4
Service Design 167, 176-80, 185, 188-92, 195-6, 198, 201-6
Service Desk 10, 17, 71, 79, 146-7, 149, 151, 156, 162, 167, 171, 173, 180, 189, 196, 202
service disruptions 143, 161
Service Improvement Plan 116, 178
Service Knowledge Management System (SKMS) 25-6, 183, 193-4, 202, 204
Service Operation 8, 20, 23, 30-1, 138, 167, 176, 180, 185-9, 191, 193-4, 196, 198, 202, 204, 206
Service Provider 31, 150, 177, 181, 183-4, 188, 190-2, 196-7, 200, 202-3, 205
Service Requests 132, 141, 146, 160-6, 169, 174, 189, 202
Service Strategy 176-80, 188, 191, 197, 199, 203, 205
Service Transition 29, 177, 180-7, 193, 198-204
services 16, 29, 41-2, 44, 62-4, 90, 126, 131-2, 138-42, 144, 146, 159-60, 166-7, 169, 171, 174
SLAs (Service Level Agreement) 26, 142-3, 146, 148, 150, 157, 162, 164, 170, 172, 182, 184, 196, 202, 205
software 73, 88, 121, 126, 182, 184-5, 190, 199
source 10-11, 35, 160
staff 5, 14, 21, 33, 41, 43, 62, 68, 84, 111, 126, 128-9, 141, 144, 155-6, 169-70
stakeholders 33, 68, 83, 132, 134, 172, 198
statement 38, 43, 46, 50, 52, 98, 106, 122-3
status 19, 26, 37, 45, 48-9, 56, 60, 66, 70-1, 81, 88, 93-4, 97, 103, 105, 115

suppliers 14, 27-8, 156, 179, 181, 183, 193, 204
support 33, 65, 70-1, 109, 126, 128-9, 134, 138-9, 144, 148, 151, 192, 196-7, 201

T

TCO (Total Cost of Ownership) 144
team 27-8, 123, 127, 142, 156, 165, 191
techniques 6, 14-16, 126, 140, 188, 191, 195-6, 204
threats 104, 200, 204-5
ticket 70-1, 85-9, 92-3, 95
types 29, 86, 88-9, 160, 163, 165, 173, 177, 180, 187

U

updates 19, 89, 95, 116-17, 202
users 7, 14, 43, 86, 89, 91-2, 151, 160, 162-4, 166-7, 169-70, 172-4, 183-4, 189, 202, 205

V

Value on Investment (VOI) 183, 199, 205
VBF (Vital Business Function) 179, 206

W

weaknesses 31, 144, 170, 204
workarounds 7, 10, 17-18, 22, 26, 78, 154, 157, 193-4, 206

LaVergne, TN USA
20 November 2010

205592LV00003B/66/P